Third Edition

Music

is FUNdamental

Fundamentals & Methods for Elementary Music

Daniel L. Steele
Central Michigan University

Kendall Hunt
publishing company

Cover images © Shutterstock, Inc.

Kendall Hunt
publishing company

www.kendallhunt.com
Send all inquiries to:
4050 Westmark Drive
Dubuque, IA 52004-1840

Contents

Why Teach Music

Imagine the world without music. How different the world would be if there were no lullabies, no Beatles' tunes, no folk songs, no Mozart operas, no hymns, no rock 'n' roll hits! Music is so pervasive in our world that it truly is difficult to imagine the world without it. Yet music's role in our public schools has often been relegated to that of a frill and viewed as being expendable in times of budget shortfalls. What is there about music that really matters, what is there about music that should be taught in our schools, and what need does music fulfill that other subjects cannot?

Music is worth knowing because it:

1. links humans in ways that only music can
2. provides a cultural map of where we are and where we have been
3. provides an avenue for aesthetic experience
4. expresses our emotions
5. provides a unique intelligence
6. nurtures creativity.

Each of the above reasons for including music as a part of what is taught in our schools is amplified below:

1. One result of the shrinking world in which we live, is that technological advances have allowed us access to the diverse musics of the world. Recordings from almost any culture and any style of music are readily available. When a recording is released, it can instantly be heard around the world. Teenagers in Los Angeles, Beijing, and London often listen to the same music at the same time.
2. The cultural heritage of any nation or people can be kept alive through its music. Folk songs and popular songs can enlighten historians' vision

of what life was like in different eras. Ethnomusicologists work to preserve folk songs and other types of music to keep traditional musics alive. Classroom teachers should incorporate the music of other cultures in social studies lessons and lead children to understand the social and cultural contexts of music.

3. Although claims have been made that music contributes to knowledge in other subject areas, or even that it makes us smarter, the study of music for music's sake is often underestimated. It is what music can do to make us have a greater understanding of, appreciation for, and skill in creating, performing, and listening to music that makes it worthy of being included in the school music program. A student cannot become fully "musically educated" without exposure to the **aesthetic** dimension of music. Aesthetics involves understanding and attending to the perceptual qualities of the music that make it unique, make it beautiful, and cause us to feel "an attachment" to the music.

4. Music can uplift us, make us feel sad, entertain us, aid in our worship, and make us want to dance. Music can elicit the entire range of emotions. A wedding seldom takes place without music to enhance our feeling of joy. Funerals are accompanied by somber music in our culture, to correspond with the feeling of grief. Rhythm and blues has such a danceable beat that it is difficult to refrain from dancing, or at least tapping our feet. Music and the other arts affect our emotions in ways that other subjects cannot. One of the most fundamental reactions that children have to music is that of joy. Teachers should encourage children to have fun in music class and express the joyfulness that music provides.

5. Howard Gardner, along with other leading psychologists, believes that intelligence has many facets and should no longer be thought of as relating only to cognitive skills. In *Frames of Mind: The Theory of Multiple Intelligences*, he affirms that there are seven major intelligences. The seven intelligences are linguistic, logical-mathematical, spatial, interpersonal, intrapersonal, kinesthetic, and musical. (Gardner, 1983). If we are to educate the whole child, we need to educate all of the intelligences, including music.

   Garner affirms that music intelligence is the first to emerge and it follows that music concepts can be cultivated in children at an early age.

6. The arts, more than any other subject area, nurture creativity. The very essence of all art forms is the creative component—the way the artist manipulates materials to make an original, creative statement. Creativity in music manifests itself in numerous ways. A first grader creating a two-measure rhythmic improvisation, a fifth grader creating a sound composition, or a tenth grader interpreting a Chopin piano piece, is immersed in the act of creating. It is difficult to imagine an elementary music lesson that does not involve creativity stemming from the teacher as well as from the students.

Who Should Teach Elementary Music

In order for children to have quality music instruction, it is recommended that music in the elementary grades be taught by a music specialist and supplemented by the classroom teacher. Many schools do have music specialists, but many times they work with the children only once or twice a week. The National Association for Music Education, NAfME, recommends that at least 12% of time in kindergarten be devoted to music instruction, and that at least 90 minutes per week of instruction in general music be provided in Kindergarten through fifth grades. (*Opportunity-to-Learn Standards for Music Instruction*, 2015). Very few schools provide the recommended amount of time with a music specialist. However, music teachers can work closely with classroom teachers and provide ideas for supplemental instruction. Most elementary classroom teachers realize the importance of music in the classroom, but many feel inadequate to teach music. However, if classroom teachers have a positive attitude toward teaching music, the students will realize that and often imitate it. The basal series books contain helpful lesson plans, companion CD sets for accompaniment for each song, as well as supplemental listening lessons. The most recent editions are on-line and include many video examples. Internet sources such as YouTube.com provide countless song examples with great animation, as well as classroom videos incorporating current music methodologies.

What Should Be Taught

The elementary general music curriculum should include study of all of the elements of music: rhythm, melody, harmony, form, timbre, and dynamics and expression. Concepts, based on each element, should be developed in a spiral fashion so that successive teaching builds on concepts previously established. The following chapters give ideas for how this might be implemented.

The United States Congress passed the *Goals 2000: Educate America Act* in 1994. The legislation marked the first time that the federal government called for the arts, including music, to be a part of the core curriculum. Leading music educators in the country created national, voluntary content standards for music. Although voluntary, the standards were very influential and were adapted by many states as the standards for music instruction. The standards are listed below.

National Standards for Music Education

1. Singing, alone and with others, a varied repertoire of music.
2. Performing on instruments, alone and with others, a varied repertoire of music.
3. Improvising melodies, variations, and accompaniments.
4. Composing and arranging music within specified guidelines.
5. Reading and notating music.
6. Listening to, analyzing, and describing music.
7. Evaluating music and music performances.
8. Understanding relationships between music, the other arts, and disciplines outside the arts.
9. Understanding music in relation to history and culture.*

---

* From *National Standards for Arts Education: What Every Child Should Know and Be Able To Do In the Arts*. (Reston, VA: Music Educators National Conference, 1994).

New national Core Music Standards were released in 2014. Whereas the 1994 standards focused on skills and knowledge, the focus of the newer standards is on understanding the artistic processes of creating, performing, and responding to music, with the goal of leading learners to music literacy. A key component of the new standards was titled *enduring understandings*. The following show the anticipated understandings for the realms of creating, performing, and responding as well as enduring understandings that connect the three areas.

Creating

1. The creative ideas, concepts, and feelings that influence musicians' work emerge from a variety of sources.
2. Musicians' creative choices are influenced by their expertise, context, and expressive content.
3. Musicians evaluate, and refine their work through openness to new ideas, persistence, and the application of appropriate criteria.
4. Musicians' presentation of creative work is the culmination of a process of creation and communication.

Performing

1. Performers' interest in and knowledge of musical works, understanding of their own technical skill, and the context for a performance influence the selection of repertoire.
2. Analyzing creators' context and how they manipulate elements of music provides insight into their intent and informs performance.
3. Performers make interpretive decisions based on their understanding of context and expressive intent.
4. To express their musical ideas, musicians analyze, evaluate, and refine their performance over time through openness to new ideas, persistence, and the application of appropriate criteria.
5. Musicians judge performance based on criteria that vary across time, place and cultures.
6. The context and how a work is presented influence the audience response.

Responding

1. Individuals' selection of musical works is influenced by their interests, experiences, understandings, and purposes.
2. Response to music is informed by analyzing context (social, cultural, and historical) and how creators and performers manipulate the elements of music.
3. Through their use of elements and structures of music, creators and performers provide clues to their expressive content.
4. The personal evaluation of musical works and performances is informed by analysis, interpretation, and established criteria.

Connecting

1. Musicians connect their personal interests, experiences, ideas, and knowledge to creating, performing, and responding.
2. Understanding connections to varied contexts and daily life enhances musicians' creating, performing, and responding.

Each of the above enduring understandings is accompanied by an *essential* question and grade level expectations are also included for each understanding. For a complete listing of the Core Music Standards for PreK-8 visit http://www .nafme.org/wp-content/uploads/2014/06/Core-Music-Standards-PreK-81.pdf.

Chapter References

Gardner, Howard. *Frames of Mind: The theory of Multiple Intelligences*. New York: Basic Books, 1983.

Core Music Standards (Pre-K-8). Accessed at http://www.nafme.org/wp-content/ uploads/2014/06/Core-Music-Standards-PreK-81.pdf.

National Standards for Arts Education: What Every Child Should Know and Be Able To Do In the Arts. Reston, VA: Music Educators National Conference, 1994.

Opportunity to Learn Standards for Music Instruction: Grades PreK-12. Reston, VA: National Association for Music Education, 2015. Accessed on-line at http:// www.nafme.org/wp-content/files/2015/01/OTL-draft-Jan-2-2015.pdf.

Rhythm 2

The world is comprised of movements of the earth around the sun, tides that rise and fall, and seasons that change. The fact that we are living implies movement: our hearts beat, we breathe in air and exhale it, and we walk from place to place. All of these movements represent rhythm. *Rhythm*, in music, can be defined as the underlying movement of music through time, made up of regular or irregular pulses. Because rhythm is so closely connected to the act of living, it is often considered the most important element of music. Rhythm encompasses a broad range of music concepts including beat, tempo, duration, meter, and syncopation.

Steady Beat

The basic, underlying pulse of the music is referred to as ***steady beat***. Steady beat can be considered the heartbeat of music because it is a recurring, consistent beat throughout a piece of music. Because steady beat is the most basic rhythm concept, it is often the first concept taught to children. When teaching children, we emphasize the same concept in many different ways so that children can internalize the idea and gain beat competence. Steady beat can be demonstrated by marching, walking, clapping to the beat, playing rhythm instruments to the beat, etc. Icons, or visual images, also help children understand musical concepts. An icon for steady beat is equidistant lines in a box.

(Activities related to steady beat include 2:1 through 2:9 in the book and accompanying video clips).

No Beat

While most Western music has a steady beat, there are types of music that do not feature a steady, recurring pulse. Although such music has rhythm, we say that there is ***no beat***. An example of a type of music with no beat is Gregorian chant. The sacred text was considered the most

(Activities related to no beat include 2:7 and 2:8 in the book and accompanying video clips).

important aspect of the music and the rhythm was determined by the flow of the text instead of being based on a recurring pulse. Other examples of pieces without a steady beat include some electronic pieces, and pieces where fermatas are used extensively. The icon used for no beat is a box without lines.

Tempo

Tempo is the speed of the beat. With young children we use the terms fast and slow to describe tempo. Eventually, these terms are replaced by the Italian designations for tempo such as *Adagio*, meaning in a leisurely manner, or *Presto*, meaning quick or rapid, etc. It is important to note that, while children often prefer pieces with a fast tempo, they also need movement experiences with slow tempo in order to develop beat competence. Initial experiences with slow tempo often result in children getting to the beat too quickly, and having difficulty in moving gracefully to the beat. As is so often the case in music, practicing does help! The icon for fast tempo is a box with lines close together.

To indicate slow tempo, a box with lines further apart is used to signify that more time occurs between each beat.

Getting faster (accelerando) and ***getting slower*** (ritardando) are aspects of tempo changes. Children should engage in movement activities that show their understanding of music getting faster or slower. The icon for getting faster is a box with lines getting closer together.

Getting slower is represented by a box with lines getting further apart.

(Activities relating to fast and slow include 2:9 and 2:10 in the book and accompanying video clips).

(Activities relating to getting faster or slower include 2:11 and 2:12 in the book and accompanying video clips).

Duration

Duration refers to the length of a sound (shown in notation with notes) or a silence (shown in notation with rests). Partly because children have a faster heartbeat than adults, they perceive length differently. To a young child, a quarter note represents a long sound. An eighth note is commonly used to represent a short sound. Music educators have developed various types of duration syllables to simplify music reading. In this text, a quarter note will be given the name *ta* and represented by a vertical line.

ta

Each eighth note will be called *ti* and represented by a vertical line with a flag.

ti

If two eighth notes occur together, two vertical lines with a **beam**, or horizontal line joining them, will be used.

ti   ti

Sixteenth notes are represented with two beams if two or more occur together or with two flags to indicate a single sixteenth note.

ti   ri   ti   ri

A half note is written in standard notation and is called ta-a.

ta - a

A listing of other duration syllables can be found on page 12.

(Activities relating to duration include Lessons 2:13 to 2:18 in the book and accompanying video clips).

Meter

The number of beats in a *measure* of music, the distance from one bar line to the next, and which beats are accented forms the basis of *meter*. Before students are expected to understand meter signatures, they should have ample opportunity to listen to music and determine if the music moves in 2's or 3's. The pattern of the accents determines the meter. If the music moves in 2's (or multiples thereof) we term the music duple. Every second beat is accented in duple.

If the music moves in 3's, it is referred to as triple, and every third beat is accented.

The *meter signature*, or time signature, is made up of the numbers that follow the key signature in notated music. There are two numbers, the top one indicates the number of beats per measure, and the bottom number indicates what kind of a note gets one beat. The bottom number is equivalent to a denominator of a fraction, with one being the constant numerator. Thus, if there is a four on the bottom, a quarter note (1/4)

gets one beat; if there is an 8 on the bottom an eighth note (1/8)

gets a beat, etc. Regardless of what kind of note gets a beat, the ratio of a half note to a quarter note (2:1) or a quarter note to an eighth (2:1) stays the same. For each type of note, there is an equivalent *rest*. A rest indicates silence. The following chart shows note and rest equivalents:

(Lesson 2:19 relates to accents in 2's or 3's).

Notes

| whole | halves | quarters | eighths | sixteenths |

Rests

| whole | halves | quarters | eighths | sixteenths |

A dot after any note adds one-half of the value of the note. The following examples show the time value of a dotted note:

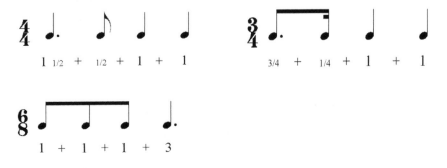

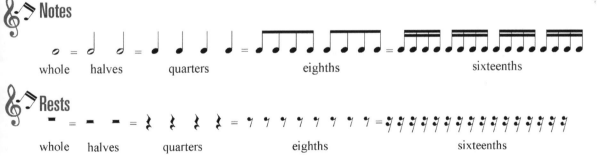

The most common meter has a 4 on top (4 beats in a measure) and a 4 on the bottom (a quarter note gets a beat). Because this meter is so prevalent, sometimes a C is used as the meter signature, meaning **common time**, instead of the Arabic numerals. See the example below.

Similarly, a meter signature of C with a line through it, resembling a cent sign, signifies **cut time**, which represents meter with both the top and bottom numbers being a 2. See the example below.

Meter can be considered as **simple meter** or **compound meter**. In simple meter the basic beat is subdivided into two equal parts. The following examples show simple meter with two eighth notes grouped together to represent simple meter.

In compound meter, the beat or pulse is subdivided into three equal parts. Three eighth notes are grouped together in compound meter as shown in the following examples.

The preceding example illustrates a note with a **tie**. A tied note is shown with a curved line over or under two notes that are the same pitch. The note is sounded once and held for the duration of the two notes. The tied note above would be sounded for 4 beats.

A curved line over or under two notes that are different pitches is called a **slur**. A slur indicates that the notes should be smooth and connected.

The example below shows a *fermata* over a note. A fermata indicates that a note is to be held longer than its normal duration. A solo performer, or the conductor of an ensemble, decides the length of time to hold a fermata.

Each measure in a piece of music must be a complete measure, with the exception of the first and last measures. A piece of music may have an incomplete measure at the beginning. When this occurs the notes before the first bar line are referred to as *pickup notes*. The duration of the pickup note or notes is taken from the last measure of the piece. So if a piece of music is in common time and the pickup notes equal one beat, the final measure of the piece would have only three beats instead of the usual four.

Regular meter implies that the music is duple or triple. *Irregular meter* results when there is a combination of 2's and 3's in one measure. For example, 5/4 meter would either consist of two beats plus three beats or three beats plus two beats depending on where the accents occur.

(Activity 2:20 relates to Irregular Meter; Meter worksheets can be found on pages 16-18)

Syncopation

Unexpected accents in music produce *syncopation*. We normally expect an accent to be on the strong beat of the measure. The strongest beat is the first beat, often called the downbeat. Syncopation results when the accent is shifted to a weak beat, or a weak part of the beat. This occurs when a) a note is tied over to the strong beat, b) when there is a rest on the strong beat, or c) when stress is given to a weak beat or weak part of a beat. See the examples that follow.

Not syncopated:

Syncopated: a. A note tied to a strong beat.

b. A rest on a strong beat.

c. Accent on a weak part of the beat.

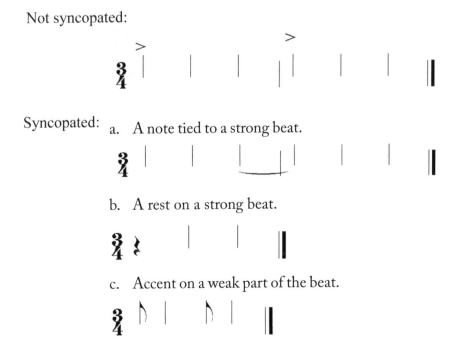

(Activity 2:21 relates to Syncopation).

Duration Syllable Chart

There is not a universally accepted system of duration syllables for common rhythm patterns. The following chart consists of recommended syllables for use with the Kodály method in America. Consistency is more important than exact syllables used and individual teachers may prefer to use syllables other than those suggested. Ta and ti ti appear at the top of the chart because they are the first to be taught.

Stick Notation	Syllable Name	Note Value	Note Name
		ta		Quarter
	ti ti		Two eighths
	ta-a		Half
	ta-a-a-a		Whole
	ti-ri-ti-ri (ti-di-ti-di)		Four Sixteenths
	ti ti-ri (ti ti-di)		Eighth, two sixteenths
	ti-ri ti (ti-di ti)		Two sixteenths, Eighth
	syn-co-pa (ti ta ti)		Eighth, Quarter, Eighth
	ta-i ti		Dotted quarter, Eighth
	ti ta-i		Eighth, Dotted quarter
	tim-di	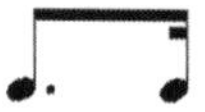	Dotted eighth, Sixteenth
	ti-di di		Sixteenth, Eighth, Sixteenth
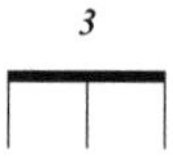	tri-ple-ti		Triplet
	rest		Quarter rest
	pet		Eighth rest

Rhythmic Competency

Rhythmic competence is an essential skill for music teachers. The following exercise is useful for demonstrating rhythmic competence. The goal is to maintain a steady beat throughout while chanting the appropriate duration syllables to common rhythm patterns. Your instructor will provide the duration syllables, based either on the Kodály method or the Gordon approach. You will use a movement to the steady beat while chanting the syllables. (Examples may include tapping the beat with one hand and the duration syllables with the other hand while chanting the syllables; marching to the beat while clapping and chanting the duration syllables; or tapping your chest while chanting the duration syllables).

Example:

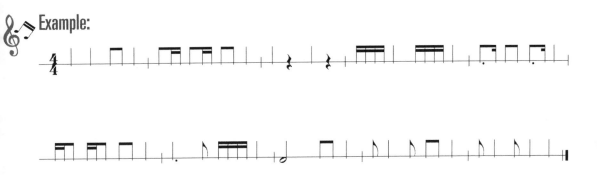

Rhythmic Echo Assignment

Before elementary students are asked to clap rhythms by themselves, they need to practice echoing rhythm patterns that the teacher claps. For this assignment you are asked to:

1. Create eight measures of rhythm patterns in 4/4 meter using the following patterns at least once:

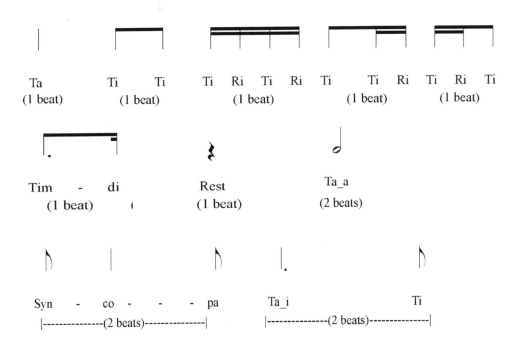

2. You will be asked to clap one measure at a time while saying the duration syllables, then gesture to the class to begin echoing on the next beat.

3. When the class finishes echoing a measure, you clap and say the next measure, beginning on the next beat, etc.

4. Prepare two copies, one for you as you present and one for your instructor.

Things to consider as you practice:

Make sure you clap for each note stem. For example, Ti Ri Ti Ri, four sixteenth notes, needs to have four claps.

Make sure the rhythm of syn-co-pa is clapped so that "co" is one entire beat, and the other syllables are a half beat (short long short).

For the dotted quarter eighth pattern, make sure that "ta" receives one entire beat and "i" a half beat.

Notes and Rests Worksheet

Match each note in the left hand column with its corresponding rest in the right column by drawing a line to it.

𝅝	𝄽
𝅗𝅥	𝄼
𝅘𝅥	𝄾
𝅘𝅥𝅮	𝄻
𝅘𝅥𝅯	𝄿

Meter Worksheets

A. Each measure below is incomplete. For each measure, add **one** note or rest that would complete the measure.

B. Add barlines to the following examples based on the given meter signature.

C. Determine the correct meter signature for the following examples. Use the most common meter that will work (for example, 4/4 instead of 8/8).

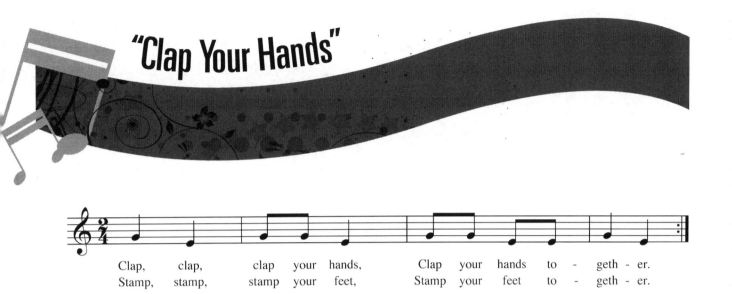

"Clap Your Hands"

Clap,   clap,   clap   your   hands,   Clap   your   hands   to - geth - er.
Stamp,   stamp,   stamp   your   feet,   Stamp   your   feet   to - geth - er.

LESSON 2:1   Version One of "Clap Your Hands"

Concept: Steady beat recognition

Objective: Students will clap, stamp, and play rhythm sticks to the steady beat with a reasonable degree of accuracy.

Materials: VIDEO 2:1
> Rhythm sticks for each child

Procedures and Strategies: Explain that a steady beat is a sound that is repeated over and over. Compare steady beat to a heartbeat. Help children find their heartbeat and elicit volunteers to demonstrate the speed of their heartbeat (with sound of their choice) to the class. Discuss other objects that have a steady beat.

Movement: Let children watch the VIDEO clip, then clap or stamp along to the steady beat images as the song is played.

Playing Instruments: Distribute rhythm sticks, repeat the VIDEO clip and ask students to perform the steady beat on the sticks as the song is played.

Extensions: Encourage children to create new verses with corresponding movements to reinforce the beat. (Nod your head, touch your toes, etc.)

"A Sailor Went to Sea"

A sail-or went to sea, sea, sea. To see what he could see, see, see. But
A sail-or went to chop, chop, chop. To see what he could chop, chop, chop. But
A sail-or went to knee, knee, knee. To see what he could knee, knee, knee. But
A sail-or went to sea, chop, knee. To see what he could see, chop, knee. But

all that he could see, see, see was the bot-tom of the deep blue sea, sea, sea.
all that he could chop, chop, chop was the bot-tom of the deep blue chop, chop, chop.
all that he could knee, knee, knee was the bot-tom of the deep blue knee, knee, knee.
all that he could see, chop, knee was the bot-tom of the deep blue sea, chop, knee.

LESSON 2:2

Concept: Steady beat reinforcement

Objective: Students will clap and march to the beat with a reasonable degree of accuracy.

Materials: VIDEO 2:2

Procedures and Strategies: Teach 1st verse by whole song method and show VIDEO clip. Instruct students to clap along with the beat as visuals are shown. Add other verses until all are learned.

Movement Game:

- 🎵 **1st verse:** March in place to the beat and salute on the words "sea, sea, sea" and "see, see, see."
- 🎵 **2nd verse:** Clap to the beat and "chop" hands one over the other on the words "chop, chop, chop."
- 🎵 **3rd verse:** March the beat and "chop" a raised knee on the words "knee, knee, knee."
- 🎵 **4th verse:** March the beat and salute on "sea," chop hands on "chop" and chop knee on "knee."

Extensions: Do movement game above and do not sing on "sea, sea, sea," etc. but perform the actions. Reinforce that the movements correspond with the steady beat.

"Stamping Land"

I trav - elled far a - cross the sea, I met a man and old was he. "Old
man," I said, "where do you live?" and this is what he told me.

"Fol - low me to stamp - ing land, stamp - ing land, stamp - ing land.
"Fol - low me to clap - ping land, clap - ping land, clap - ping land.
"Fol - low me to tip - toe land, tip - toe land, tip - toe land.

If you wish to live with me, fol - low me to stamp - ing land."
All who wish to live with me, fol - low me to clap - ping land."
All who wish to live with me, flo - low me to tip - toe land."

LESSON 2:3

Concept: Steady Beat reinforcement

Objective: Students will accurately clap, stamp, and tiptoe to the beat. Students will clap and stamp loudly (*forte*) and tiptoe quietly (*piano*).

Materials: VIDEO 2:3a and 2:3b
　　　　　Craft sticks (popsicle type)

Procedures and Strategies: Children will learn the chorus of the song by watching the **VIDEO 2:3a** and singing it with the teacher. Introduce steady beat movements of clapping, stamping, tiptoeing to correspond with the text and visuals during the refrain.

VIDEO 2:3b is the same song, but ta symbols have been superimposed over the steady beat images on each refrain. Have children watch and clap along with each ta (beat).

Distribute craft sticks (at least 16) to each child. Sing the refrain for children and ask them to place one stick for every ta they hear. (You may want to suggest they arrange them in rows of 4 or 8). Repeat (and assist) as needed until children have mapped the beat.

Discuss loud sounds and quiet sounds with the children. (Although we use the musical term "soft," children tend to think of soft as relating to texture, i.e. a soft bunny, and the term "quiet" is more indicative of the sound level). Lead students to discover that loud, or *forte* sounds are appropriate for clapping land and stamping land, but quiet, or *piano* sounds are more appropriate for tiptoeing.

"Jack-O-Lantern"

Jack-o'-lan-tern, Jack-o'-lan-tern, You are such a fun-ny sight. As you
You were once a yel-low pump-kin grow-ing on a stur-dy vine. Now you

sit there in the win - dow, Look - ing out at the night.
are a Jack - o' - lan - tern, See the can - dle - light shine!

LESSON 2:4

Concept: Steady beat reinforcement*

Objective: Children will sway to the steady beat and point to ta symbols as the beat occurs.

Materials: VIDEO 2:4a, 2:4b, and 2:4c
Large, pumpkin shaped cutout for each child.
Cuisenaire rods (approximately 1 inch long)

Procedures and Strategies: Teach the song and view **VIDEO 2:4a** which has a jack-o'-lantern lit on each beat. Repeat song while viewing **VIDEO 2:4b** which shows ta symbols superimposed over the jack-o'-lantern images. Instruct the children to sway to the beat as they sing.

Extensions: Give the children a pumpkin pattern and instruct them to draw a jack-o'-lantern and use Cuisenaire rods to represent "Ta" symbols for the mouth, nose, eyes, etc. Demonstrate with a rod that "Ta" could be a diagonal, horizontal, or vertical line. One such example is:

As they sing the song again, ask children to point to a rod (ta symbol) on their pumpkin for each beat.

When students can internalize the beat, discuss that some places in the song have two words to one beat. Clap the beat while singing the song, and ask students to indicate places where they heard two sounds to one beat. If we clap on every syllable of the song, we are clapping the **word rhythm** (or melodic rhythm). Direct students to clap the word rhythm with you as they sing the song. View **VIDEO 2:4c** which shows the jack-o-lantern flash off and on to the word rhythm.

*Kodály emphasized that each new concept be reinforced many times in order for children to internalize it. Thus, many lessons emphasize the same concept in different ways.

Song Credit: "Jack-O'-Lantern words from *Songs for the Little Child*, by Clara Belle baker, 1949.

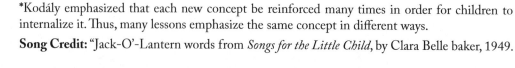

"Bee, Bee, Bumblebee"

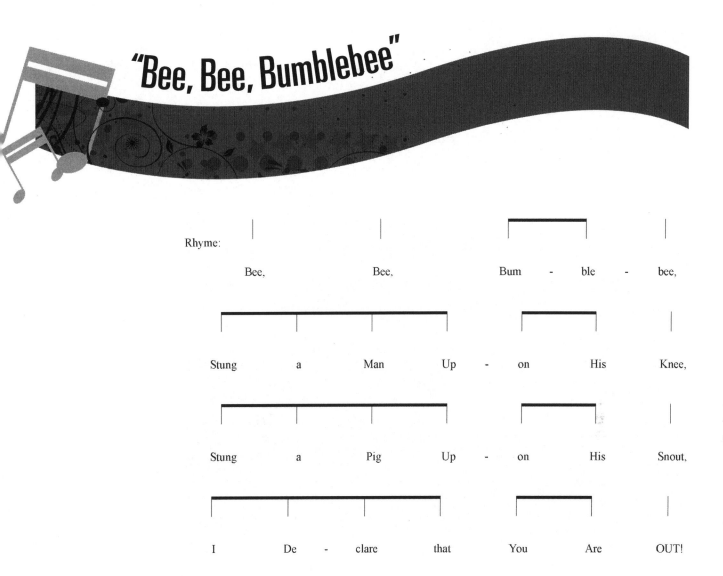

Rhyme:

Bee,   Bee,   Bum - ble - bee,

Stung   a   Man   Up - on   His   Knee,

Stung   a   Pig   Up - on   His   Snout,

I   De - clare   that   You   Are   OUT!

LESSON 2:5

Concept: Steady Beat Reinforcement

Objective: Students will demonstrate understanding of steady beat by tapping the beat of the rhyme and by playing games that show steady beat competence.

Materials: VIDEO 2:5
> Bee puppet (purchased or teacher-constructed)

Procedures and Strategies: Ask children for examples of steady beat (heart beat, clock ticking, etc.). View VIDEO clip and ask children what they observed about the images. (They represented a steady beat). Play the clip again and ask children to clap to the beat.

Extension: Game: Children are seated in a circle. Teach "Bee, Bee, Bumblebee" chant by saying it while tapping each child, to the beat, with a bee puppet. After the word "Out" the teacher goes to the next child and creates a series of buzzes in various rhythm patterns. (Such as "Bzzz, Bzzz, Bzzz, Bzzz, Bzzz" for ta, ta, ti ti, ta. Children echo the buzz pattern and the child who was "buzzed" takes the bee puppet and taps children as the chant is repeated.

Game Variation: Children are arranged in groups of four. Three of the children sit on the floor forming a circle with outstretched legs and with their feet touching. The fourth child, the "bee catcher," is in the center and taps a foot for each beat of the rhyme. The foot that is tapped on the word "Out" is taken out of the circle. Continue until one foot is left and that child becomes the bee catcher.

Procedures and Strategies: Explain that many songs and poems have a steady beat, but that some do not. If a steady beat cannot be detected, we refer to that song or poem as having **no beat**. Draw icons to represent steady beat and no beat and explain that the vertical lines represent the beat, the lack of lines represents no beat.

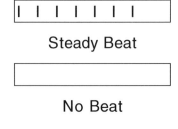

Steady Beat

No Beat

View the VIDEO clip and ask students what they noticed about the images. (They were random and were not steady). Discuss that the images were not steady because the poem does not have a steady beat. Ask students to clap a random (not steady) beat while the VIDEO is viewed again. Ask a few students to select instruments to portray the sound of wind. Rehearse random sounds and then add sounds as VIDEO is played a final time.

"The Wind Blew East"

ARR. BY JAMES ROOKER

LESSON 2:6

Concept: Steady Beat and No beat

Objective: Students will accompany the A section of "The Wind Blew East" with random beats and use steady beat accompaniment for the B section with a reasonable degree of accuracy.

Materials: VIDEO 2:6
> Tambourines and hand drums

Procedures and Strategies: View the VIDEO clip and ask the students if they noticed any changes in the beat of the song. (Section A is not steady, Section B has a steady beat). Distribute tambourines to a few students and ask them to demonstrate random beats which are not steady. Distribute hand drums to other students and ask them to demonstrate a steady beat after your cue. As the VIDEO clip is played again, have the tambourines play on Section A and the hand drums on Section B.

Assessment: Play several excerpts, some with a steady beat and some without. If students think there is a steady beat, they clap their hands to the beat. If they do not hear a steady beat they keep their hands still.

"The Elephant Song"

One el-e-phant went out to play, Out on a spi-der's web one day.
Two el-e-phants went out to play, Out on a spi-der's web one day.

He had such e-nor-mous fun, He called for an-oth-er el-e-phant to come.
They had such e-nor-mous fun, They called for an-oth-er el-e-phant to come.

LESSON 2:7

Concept: Steady Beat or No Beat, Ta Reinforcement

Objective: Students will determine whether "The Elephant Song" has a steady beat or no beat, will clap to the beat, and will draw ta symbols in the air to the beat.

Materials: VIDEO 2:7

Procedures and Strategies: Ask students to listen to the song to determine whether or not a steady beat can be felt. Second time through ask them to clap the beat along with the VIDEO images. After they know the song, half of the class sings while the other half "draws" ta symbols in the air (corresponding to the beat).

Game: Try the following movement sequence with the children (Works best with 2nd graders or older).

One child is "elephant" and has hands on hips:

- 𝄞 **Beat 1**: Step forward with left foot
- 𝄞 **Beat 2**: Step forward with right foot

- 𝄞 **Beat 3**: Place left heel forward and to the left
- 𝄞 **Beat 4**: Place left foot even with right foot
- 𝄞 **Beat 5**: Place right heel forward and to the right
- 𝄞 **Beat 6**: Place right foot even with left foot
- 𝄞 **Beat 7**: Squat
- 𝄞 **Beat 8**: Stand up.

Continue the sequence throughout the song.

The child chooses another "elephant" to join by calling: "Susie, elephant" (MM SS M) and then class sings "Two elephants went out to play . . ." Continue until a long line of elephants, or until all have had a turn. At end of game, teacher calls: "Sit down, elephants" (MM SS M) and the "elephants" go back to their seats.

"If You're Happy"

If you're hap-py and you know it, clap your hands, (clap, clap) If you're
hap-py and you know it, clap your hands, (clap, clap) If you're
hap-py and you know it, then your face will sure-ly show it, If you're
hap-py and you know it, clap your hands (clap, clap).

2. tap your toe, (tap, tap)
3. nod your head, (nod, nod)
4. do all three (at once)

LESSON 2:8

Concepts: Tempo: Fast; Steady Beat

Objective: Students will demonstrate beat accuracy at a fast tempo by clapping, tapping, and nodding to the beat of "If You're Happy."

Materials: VIDEO 2:8
Pictures of fast and slow objects
Hand drum

Procedures and Strategies: Show pictures and discuss things that move fast or slow. (Use comparisons such as an airplane and a hot air balloon, pushing a baby stroller and riding a bicycle, etc.). Demonstrate icons for fast (beats close together) and slow (beats far apart). Play steady beat patterns at a fast tempo on the hand drum and ask students to repeat. Repeat using a slow tempo. Ask students to watch the VIDEO clip and do the motions that the words indicate (clap, tap, nod, do all three). Discuss that the tempo was fairly fast. Sing the song at an even faster tempo and determine if the students can keep an accurate beat.

"Somer, Ade" ("Summer Goodbye)"

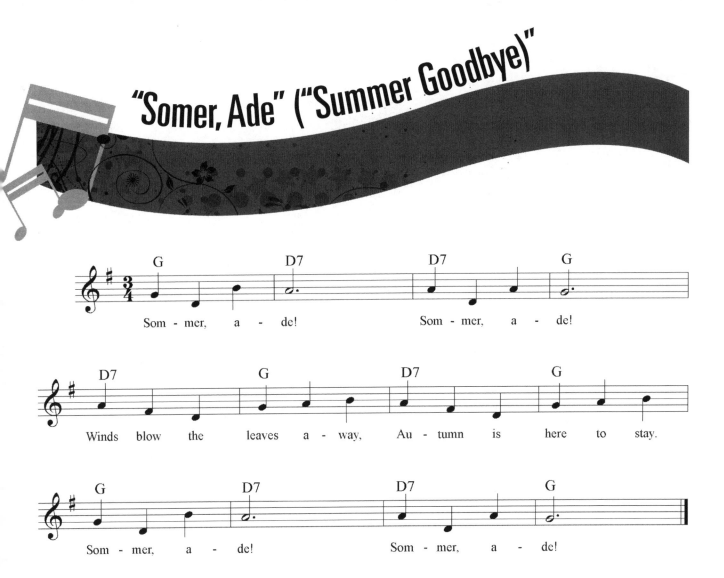

LESSON 2:9

Concept: Tempo: Slow; Accented and Unaccented Beats

Objective: Students will sway to the accented beat of "Somer Ade" and accurately clap on the accented beats and pat on the unaccented beats.

Materials: VIDEO 2:9

> **2** Rhythm instruments: one louder than the other (such as hand drum and sand blocks)

Procedures: Sing "Somer Ade" for the students and ask whether it was fast or slow. (Slow). Explain that it is lullaby-like and discuss that lullabies are slow because they are intended to "lull" the baby to sleep. View the VIDEO clip which shows falling leaves. Ask why the leaf was larger on beat one and smaller on beats two and three. (Beat one is the accented or strong beat, and beats two and three are unaccented or weak beats). As the VIDEO clip is viewed a second time, ask the students to sway to the accented beat. Repeat the song while clapping on the accented beat and patting on beats two and three. Add rhythm instrument accompaniment with a louder instrument on beat one and a softer instrument for beats two and three.

Extension: Students improvise a dance to go along with the song. Suggested movements could be pretending to be falling leaves, rocking a baby, etc.

"The Old Gray Cat"

The	old	gray	cat	is	sleep - ing,	sleep - ing,	sleep - ing,	The
The	lit - tle	mice	are	creep - ing,	creep - ing,	creep - ing,	The
The	lit - tle	mice	are	nib - bling,	nib - bling,	nib - bling,	The
The	lit - tle	mice	are	sleep - ing,	sleep - ing,	sleep - ing,	The
The	old	gray	cat	comes	creep - ing,	creep - ing,	creep - ing,	The
The	lit - tle	mice	all	scam - per,	scam - per,	scam - per,	The

old	gray	cat	is	sleep - ing	in	the	house._____
lit - tle	mice	are	creep - ing	through	the	house._____
lit - tle	mice	are	nib - bling	in	the	house._____
lit - tle	mice	are	sleep - ing	in	the	house._____
old	gray	cat	comes	creep - ing	through	the	house._____
lit - tle	mice	all	scam - per	through	the	house._____

LESSON 2:10

Concept: Fast and Slow

Objective: Students will act out "The Old Gray Cat" using appropriate tempo for each verse.

Materials: VIDEO 2:10

Movement Game: Teach the first verse of the song by rote. View VIDEO clip of the cat and mice images and the "metronome" that shows the beat for each verse. Discuss why some verses were faster and some slower. (The text of the song dictates). Sing entire song and exaggerate faster and slower portions. The class then acts out the song; one child is the old gray cat and the others are mice. Make sure tempo changes are observed.

"See The Pony Galloping"

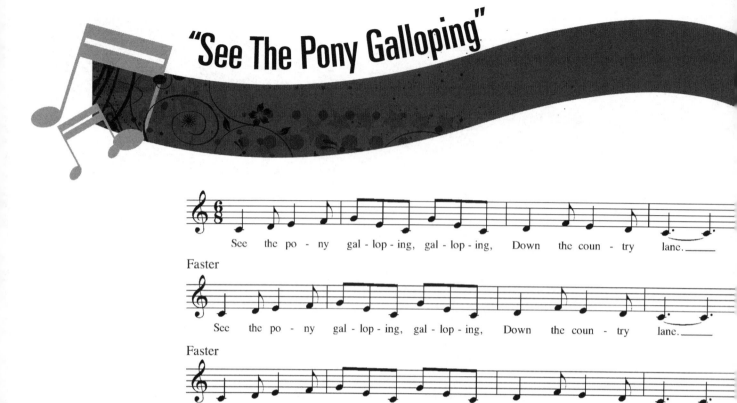

LESSON 2:11

Concept: Fast and Slow

Objective: Students will demonstrate understanding of fast and slow by galloping faster or slower as the tempo changes.

Materials: VIDEO 2:11
Metronome

Procedures and Strategies: Discuss objects that are fast (race cars, airplanes, motor boats, jogger) and objects that are slow (turtle, hot air balloon, snail, person walking). Explain that songs can be fast or slow depending on the speed of the beat. Demonstrate fast beats and slow beats with a Metronome and have class clap to the different tempi. Ask children to listen for faster and slower portions as they view the VIDEO clip which shows a pony galloping to the beat. Discuss that the beginning of the song gets faster and faster and that the song slows toward the end. Teach the song by rote. Have the children pretend to be ponies and gallop faster as the song speeds up, and gallop slower at the end.

"Bye Baby Bunting"

Bye ba - by bunt - ing Dad - dy's gone a hunt - ing to

catch a lit - tle rab - bit skin to wrap the ba - by bunt - ing in.

LESSON 2:12   Version One of "Bye Baby Bunting"

Concept: Long and short (preparation for ta and ti ti)

Objective: Students will demonstrate understanding of long and short sounds by labeling objects as long or short and identifying when they hear long sounds or short sounds.

Materials: VIDEO 2:12a and 2:12b

Pictures of long and short objects for discussion (i.e., long and short crayon, ruler, balloon)

Procedures and Strategies: Use pictures of long and short objects for discussion. Teach the song via the Whole Song method. View the **VIDEO 2:12a** clip that shows images on the steady beat and ask children to clap the beat and sing the song. Next, the teacher sings the song phrase by phrase and asks the children to listen for places where they hear shorter sounds (two sounds to a beat). Children can clap the beat as you do this. Identify the places where two sounds occur to the beat as short sounds, whereas, one sound to the beat represents a long sound. Ask the children to clap to every sound they hear, whether long or short as **VIDEO 2:12b** is shown. (A separate image is shown for each short and long sound).

"Rover"

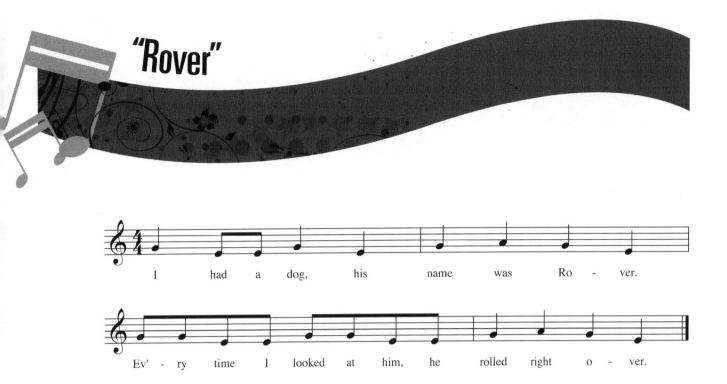

Lyrics under the music:
I had a dog, his name was Ro - ver.
Ev' - ry time I looked at him, he rolled right o - ver.

LESSON 2:13

Concept: Ta and ti ti

Objective: Students will demonstrate understanding of ta and ti ti by correctly labeling patterns and by creating a four beat pattern that uses ta and ti ti.

Materials: VIDEO 2:13
Paper and pencils
Chalk board

Procedures and Strategies: View the VIDEO clip. Ask the children why some of the dogs on the poster were long and some short. Introduce a long sound as **ta** and a short sound as **ti**. Explain that short sounds often occur in pairs and because there are two sounds they are called **ti ti**. Show the symbol for ti ti. On the board, isolate patterns of ta and ti ti that occur in the song and ask the children to echo as you clap them and say ta or ti ti. Then have the children create 2 or 3 patterns of their own. Each pattern should have four beats and include at least one ti ti. Children practice clapping patterns that they created, and those that other children created.

Movement: As you and class sing the song again, instruct students to take a long step for each **ta** sound and short steps for each **ti** sound.

"Pease Porridge Hot"

Pease por - ridge hot, Pease por - ridge cold,

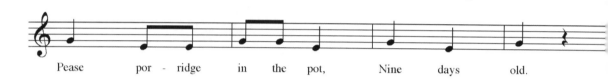

Pease por - ridge in the pot, Nine days old.

LESSON 2:14

Concept: Quarter rest

Objective: Students will demonstrate understanding of silence in music by covering their lips with a finger when a quarter rest occurs and by creating rhythm patterns that contain quarter rests.

Materials: VIDEO 2:14
Chalkboard

Procedures and Strategies: Teach the song by rote. Ask students to view the VIDEO clip. Repeat the clip while children quietly tap the beat (Tapping two fingers in the palm of a hand works well). Ask students if they noticed any beats where there was silence instead of music. Explain that these silences are called rests, and they are silent just as we are silent when resting. Point out that the rests in the song are accompanied by an image of a finger covering lips as though saying "Sh." (The other images represent porridge). Repeat the VIDEO clip and ask children to cover their lips when they hear the silence.

Ask volunteers to write a four beat pattern on board that includes at least one rest. Class claps and says ta ti ti, and rest for patterns that volunteers have created.

"Bow Wow Wow"

Bow, wow, wow,   whose dog art thou?   Little Tom-my Tuck-er's dog   bow, wow, wow.

LESSON 2:15

Concept: Ta, ti ti review and Quarter Rest reinforcement

Objectives: Students will write the symbol, **Z**, for a quarter rest and create 3 beat and 4 beat patterns containing quarter rests. Students will demonstrate understanding of ta ti ti and quarter rest by accurately clapping and playing those patterns.

Materials: VIDEO 2:15a, 2:15b, and 2:15c
Paper and pencils
Stick notation of song on board
2 types of rhythm instruments such as hand drums and rhythm sticks

Procedures and Strategies: View **VIDEO 2:15a** that shows a dog image for each ta and ti and covered lips when there is no sound. This silence is called a quarter rest and can be shown by a Z. (Demonstrate on the board). View **VIDEO 2:15b** that shows ta and ti symbols and a z for the rests. Teach the song by rote. Clap several measures with ta ti ti and rests and have children echo each. (Clap and say ta or ti ti, hands touch shoulders for rest). Children create three or four beat patterns that include ta ti ti and rests. Ask for volunteers to perform their pattern.

Lead children to derive notation of "Bow Wow Wow" on board, one measure at a time. Give several children a hand drum and several children rhythm sticks. As the class sings the duration syllables again, children with a drum play on each ta, children with sticks on each ti ti. All are silent on the quarter rests. Switch instruments until all have a turn.

Extension: Create a sung ostinato on the syllable do using the following repeated pattern throughout the song:

I	I	I	Z
Bow	Wow	Wow	

Select some of the children to sing the ostinato while the rest of the class sings the song.

Game: VIDEO 2:16c View video of children playing "Bow Wow Wow" game:

Directions: Children are in a circle facing a partner..

- 𝄞 **1st phrase:** "Bow, wow, wow." Pat with both hands to the beat, three times
- 𝄞 **2nd phrase:** "Whose dog art thou?" Clap partners hands three times with the heartbeat ("Whose," "dog," "Thou.")
- 𝄞 **3rd phrase:** "Little Tommy Tucker's dog" Partners join hands and circle around.
- 𝄞 **4th phrase:** "Bow, wow, wow." Students turn half way around and face new partner.
- 𝄞 **Repeat!**

"Rain Is Falling Down"

LESSON 2:16

Concepts: Ta, ti, ti, and Z reinforcement
Singing an ostinato

Objectives: Students will notate ta, ti ti, and Z patterns contained in the song.
Students will sing accurately an ostinato pattern against the melody of the song.

Materials: VIDEO 2:16
Chalkboard
Glockenspiel or Songbells
Rain stick

Procedures and Strategies: Echo clap ta ti ti patterns as a review. Teach song by
rote. View VIDEO clip which shows an image for each ta and ti ti of the song.
Solicit volunteers to clap patterns from the song (one or two measures at a time).
Notate correct patterns on the board until notation of entire song is derived. Sing
song again with words while clapping the rhythmic pattern. Select a child to add
glockenspiel glissando (downward) on each "Rain and "Down." Add a rain stick
(a child turns it over when it stops sounding) throughout the song.

Teach ostinato pattern:　I　Z　I　Z
　　　　　　　　　　　　Mi　　Do
　　　　　　　　　　　　Rain　　Rain

Divide class and have half sing the *ostinato* while other half sings melody. Add
glockenspiel and rain stick.

Extension: This is an excellent song for teaching solfege of *mi, re,* and *do.* If children are ready hand signs can be added, use staff boards to show note placement and so forth.

Assessment: To assess understanding of ta, ti ti and Z, clap a 4 beat pattern without saying duration syllables. Student echoes the pattern and says the duration syllables.

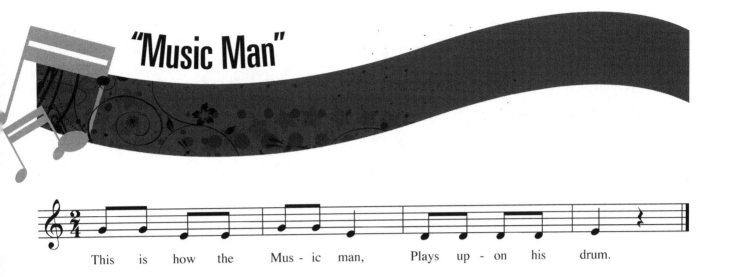

"Music Man"

This is how the Mus - ic man, Plays up - on his drum.

LESSON 2:17

Concept: Ta and ti ti reinforcement

Objective: Students will accurately echo a four beat, ta ti ti pattern by clapping and saying the correct duration syllables and by echoing a ta ti ti pattern on a hand drum.

Materials: VIDEO 2:17
           2 or 3 Hand drums

Procedures and Strategies: View **VIDEO 2:17** as preparation for song. The following steps occur on the video:

1. Teacher claps 4 beat patterns using ta, ti ti and Z and says duration syllables; children echo by clapping and saying the syllables.
2. Teacher claps 4 beat patterns without saying duration syllables; children echo without saying syllables.
3. Teacher claps patterns without saying duration syllables; children echo clap and say the duration syllables.
4. Song is sung followed by teacher clapping a ta ti ti pattern on the drum and two children echo the pattern on their drum. Children then pass it to next children and they echo next pattern, etc.

Teach song by rote. Determine ta, ti ti pattern of song and notate on board. With children seated in a circle, perform song with teacher drumming a ta, ti ti pattern and children taking turns echoing the pattern. Children who don't have the drum can play their "pretend" drum.

Extension: Give two children a hand drum and they echo the four-beat pattern simultaneously.

Meter in 2s or 3s

LESSON 2:18

Concept: Meter in 2s or 3s

Objective: Students will listen to several songs and indicate whether the song moves in 2s or 3s by clapping on the strong beat and patting on the weak beats.

Materials: **VIDEO 2:18a and 2:18b**
Songs on VIDEO: "Clap Your Hands," "Jack-o-Lantern," "Somer Ade," and "Pease Porridge Hot."
Paper and pencils

Procedures and Strategies: Ask the class to listen for the strong beat while you clap several patterns in 2 and several patterns in 3. Lead them to discover that the accent pattern for meter in 2s is:

and that the accent pattern for music in 3s is:

Ask the class to clap on the accented beat and pat on the unaccented beats while you sing several songs, exaggerating the accented beat. Ask children to write whether each song moves in 2s or 3s as they view **VIDEO 2:18a**. Discuss their answers, then view **VIDEO 2:18b** that shows images grouped in 2s or 3s with bar lines added.

"Speech Canon"

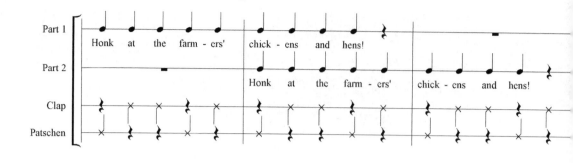

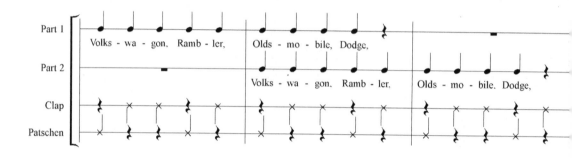

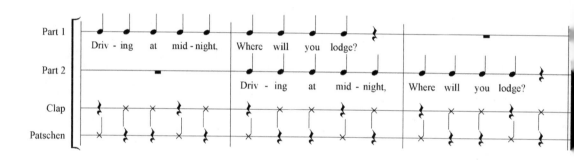

LESSON 2:19

Concept: Irregular Meter

Objective: Students will perform "Speech Canon" as a two-part canon while patting on strong beats and clapping on weak beats in 5/4 meter (3 + 2).

Materials: VIDEO 2:19
        Chalk board
        2 groups of rhythm instruments such as woodblocks and maraccas

Procedures: Teacher says the word "hippopotamus" and the phrase "strawberry jelly" emphasizing the accents. Ask students to determine which sounds like 2 + 3 beats and which sounds like 3 + 2 beats. (Hippopotamus is 2 + 3, Strawberry jelly is 3 + 2). Write each word on the board and show the accent patterns.

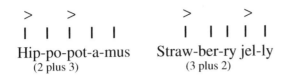

Explain that combinations of 3 beats and 2 beats per measure result in **irregular meter**. Examples of irregular meter are 5/4, 7/4, 5/2, 11/4, etc. Measures in 5/4 meter can be 3 + 2 or 2 + 3 beats. Measures in 7/4 meter can be 2 + 2 + 3, 2 + 3 + 2, or 3 + 2 + 2. Challenge students to come up with phrases that fit one of the above patterns. (For example, "strawberry jelly bellies" would be 3 + 2 + 2).

View the VIDEO clip that shows the notation and rhythmic accompaniment for "Speech Canon." When students learn the rhyme, try it as a canon as notated.

Extension: Use two groups of rhythm instruments as accompaniment. The woodblocks could take the place of the pats and maracas substitute for the claps.

"My Landlord"

LESSON 2:20

Concept: Syncopation

Objective: Students will add syncopated and un-syncopated accompaniments to "My Landlord" and will identify where syncopation occurs in the song.

Materials: VIDEO 2: 20
        Woodblocks and maracas
        Chalkboard

Procedures and Strategies: Teach the song by rote. Explain that syncopation is a term meaning unexpected accents. Syncopation adds rhythmic variety and excitement to music and is a prominent feature in jazz. Ask children where accents normally occur in various meters. (On the strong beats: beat one in 2/4, beat one in 3/4, beats one and three in 4/4, etc.). Explain that in syncopation, accents come on unexpected beats or the last half of the strong beat instead of the first half. Syncopation can result when a rest occurs on a strong beat, for example, Z I I I, when a note is tied over to a strong beat, or when a short long short pattern occurs such as an eighth, a quarter, and an eighth note. (Notate various syncopated patterns on the board).

Give three or four students a woodblock and ask them to play on beats one and three (strong beats) while the rests of the class sings the song again. Ask the students if that accompaniment was syncopated? (No). Ask what would change if the accompaniment were syncopated. (Accents would come on the weak beats). Distribute three or four maracas to students and ask them to play on the second and fourth beats (weak beats) as the song is sung again. Discuss that this time the accompaniment was syncopated.

View VIDEO that shows the notation of the song as it is sung. Guide children to find syncopation in the song.

Hand Jive Game: Students of all ages will enjoy adding the following hand jive to the song.

Everyone faces a partner.

- ♪ **Beat one**: Clap own hands
- ♪ **Beat two**: Partners clap right hands together
- ♪ **Beat three**: Clap own hands
- ♪ **Beat four**: Partners clap left hands together
- ♪ **Beat five**: Clap own hands
- ♪ **Beat six**: Partners clap hands together
- ♪ **Beat seven**: Cross hands on shoulders
- ♪ **Beat eight**: Patschen

Repeat the eight beat pattern throughout the song. Practice the hand jive first and then begin the song on beat eight when the students are ready.

Melody 3

All of the rhythmic concepts discussed in Chapter Two can exist without music. One can clap a steady beat, pat various durations, and tap a syncopated pattern, yet that is not music unless pitch is added. *Melody* refers to the highness or lowness of pitch. Music results when melody, a succession of musical pitches, is added to rhythm. Melody can also be referred to as the horizontal arrangement of pitches, or *tune* of a song. Melodic concepts include high and low, melodic direction, melodic contour, steps and skips, intervals, and scales.

High or Low

Children often confuse *high* and *low* with loud and soft. When watching television, we often say "turn it up" when we desire more volume. We really mean to "make it louder," and our misuse of the term can be confusing to children. To demonstrate high and low, a good strategy is to play a high note on the piano both at a loud and soft dynamic level and to do the same with a low note on the piano. Demonstrate to the students that the note being played loudly or softly has no bearing on the pitch—it is still a high or low note. The next step would be to use the high and low registers of a child's voice. Ask students to sing C1 (an octave above middle C) to demonstrate a high sound and Middle C to represent a low sound. The following icons are used to represent high and low:

(Activity 3:1 in the book and accompanying video clip reinforces High and Low).

↑   ↓

High   Low

Melodic Direction

Melodic direction refers to the direction in which the melody, or tune, is moving. A melody may get higher, get lower, or stay the same from one note to the next. Teachers often use hand levels to show whether the melody is rising, falling, or not changing. We use an arrow slanting upward to show pitches getting higher, an arrow slanting downward to show pitches getting lower, and a horizontal arrow to show that the pitch remains the same.

(Activities relating to Melodic Direction include 3:2 and 3:3 and accompanying video clips).

Upward   Downward   Same

Melodic Contour

The overall shape of a melody is referred to as ***melodic contour***. Contour can be shown phrase by phrase, or an entire song can be shown with a contour map. When showing the contour of a phrase, dots can be used to indicate each pitch or a line can be drawn to show the upward or downward movement. The phrase contour of "My Country 'tis of Thee" from *America* can be shown as:

(Activities related to Melodic Contour include 3:4 and 3:5 in the book and accompanying video clips).

The melodic contour of "The Hotdog Song" **p. 72** could be represented visually as:

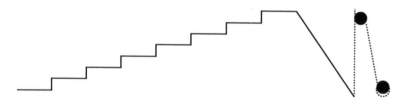

Steps and Skips

When children are first beginning to read staff notation, steps and skips should be introduced. A *step* is from one staff line to the space above or below that line, or from one staff space to the line above or below that space. A *skip* is from a space to a space on the staff or farther or from a line to a line on the staff or any farther distance. The two notes of each measure on the first staff below represent steps. Skips are shown in each measure on the second staff.

STEPS

(Steps and skips are reinforced in 3:20 in the book and accompanying video clip and on the worksheet on page 61).

SKIPS

Intervals

An *interval* is the distance from one note to the next. Intervals are counted by numbering the line or space of the first note, all lines and spaces between the two notes, and the line or space of the second note. Examples of intervals from a 2nd to an *octave* are shown on the staff below. (An octave is an interval of an eighth and the top note and bottom note of an octave have the same letter name, A to A, etc.).

(See Interval worksheet on p. 98).

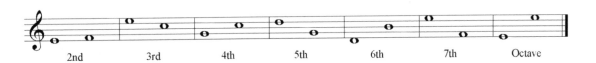

| 2nd | 3rd | 4th | 5th | 6th | 7th | Octave |

Note Names

Although the music alphabet uses only A, B, C, D, E, F, and G there are many different A's, B's, etc. on a piano. The use of the Grand Staff helps us know which A or which B to play on the piano or other instrument. For example, Middle C is notated on one *ledger line* above the bass clef, or one ledger line below the treble clef. (A ledger line is an added line above or below the clef to accommodate higher or lower notes.). Other C's are placed higher or lower on the grand staff. The fourth space of the treble clef is C an octave higher than Middle C, and the second space of the bass clef is C an octave lower than Middle C. Examine the note names of the Grand Staff below. Pneumonic devices can be used to help you remember letter names. For example, the treble clef spaces spell "FACE." The letters of the treble lines can be remembered by using the statement: "Every Good Boy Does Fine." For the spaces of the bass clef (A, C, E, G), "All Cars Eat Gas," can be used, etc.

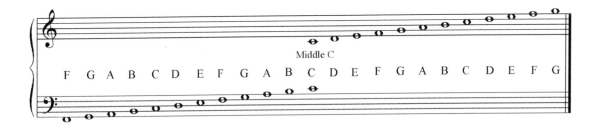

As can be seen above, the space directly above or below the clef does not need a ledger line. For example, the D below the first treble clef line does not need a ledger line, but Middle C and any lower notes do. Likewise, the G above the fifth line does not require a ledger line, but any higher notes would. See the staff below for examples of treble clef ledger line notes.

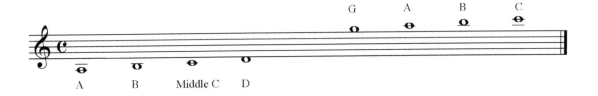

(See Note Names
Worksheet on page 59)

Ledger lines in the bass clef follow the same rules as the treble clef. Study the bass clef ledger lines below. More ledger lines can be added if lower or higher notes than those shown are needed.

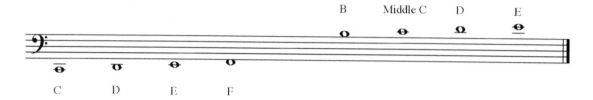

Scales

A scale is a pre-determined pattern of pitches. There are many types of scales. The most common in Western music include *major scales* and *pentatonic scales*. A major scale has eight notes that encompass an octave. It is comprised of *whole steps* and *half steps*. A keyboard can be used to better visualize the difference between whole and half steps. A half step is from one key to the next on a keyboard. A *sharp (#)* raises a note a half step, a *flat (♭)* lowers a note a half step, and a *natural (♮)* cancels the effect of a sharp or flat. Therefore, a note a half step higher than F would be called F# (or G♭). A whole step skips one key between the bottom and top notes, so a whole step higher than F would skip F# and go to G. Notice that the black keys of the keyboard are grouped in 2s and 3s. The letter C always comes before the set of two black keys and the letter F comes before the set of three black keys. The black keys are given two different letter names, one represents a raised note, called a sharp, and the other represents a lowered note, called a flat. Study the keyboard below to determine half and whole steps and to review placement of sharps and flats.

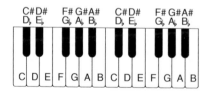

(Complete the half and whole
step exercises on page 60)

The pattern of steps making up a *major scale* is always whole, whole, half, whole, whole, whole, half. In other words, there is always a half step between notes 3 and 4 and 7 and 8, and all other intervals are whole steps. Major scales are *diatonic*, meaning that each letter name of the music alphabet (A, B, C, D, E, F, and G) is used consecutively. The last note of the major scale will be the same letter name as the first note since the major scale encompasses an octave. The keys marked with a letter name on the keyboard below form a major scale in the key of D Major.

Latin syllables, known as *solfege*, can be used to label each note of a major scale. The order of the Latin syllables is *Do, Re, Mi, Fa, So, La, Ti,* and *Do.* Major scales consist of all whole steps between pitches except between *mi-fa* (notes 3 and 4) and *ti-do* (notes 7 and 8) which are half steps.

The notation for a D Major scale appears below. Notice that F and C needed to be raised (so sharps are used) in order to have the Whole, Whole, Half,

Whole, Whole, Whole, Half relationship required for a major scale. The half steps between *mi-fa* (notes 3 to 4) and *ti-do* (notes 7 to 8) are bracketed. The Latin syllables are also shown for the scale. The first note of a major scale is *Do* regardless of the letter name, the second note is *Re*, etc.

(See Solfege worksheet on page 62)

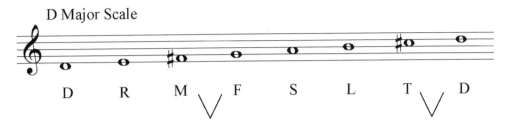

The keys marked with a letter name on the keyboard below form a D Major scale.

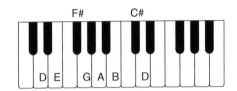

(Major scale worksheets can be found on pages 63 and 64. Activities related to the major scale include 3:4, 3:5 and 3:21 in the book and accompanying video clips, and the worksheet on pp. 63–4)

A *pentatonic scale,* as its name implies, is a five-note scale. The pentatonic scale uses notes 1, 2, 3, 5, and 6 of the major scale. (Do, Re, Mi, So, La in solfege). The smallest interval between notes is a whole step. Because there are no half steps in a pentatonic scale, children tend to match pitch better in pentatonic songs than songs using major scales. Pentatonic is also useful in improvisations, whether sung or played on instruments. The keys marked with a letter name on the keyboard below form a pentatonic scale with a key center of D.

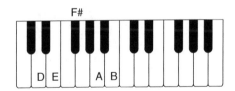

The notation for D Pentatonic appears below.

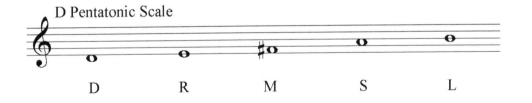

(Activity 3:17 and 3:18 in the book and accompanying video clips relate to the Pentatonic Scale).

The key of C Major always has the same notes: C, D, E, F, G, A, B, C. The key of B flat major also always has the same notes, B flat, C, D, E flat, F, G, A, B flat. Because each key consistently has the same number of sharps or flats, *key signatures* are used to quickly identify the key. A key signature is the group of sharps or flats that occur at the beginning of the treble or bass clef, immediately following the clef sign. The following rules apply to major key signatures.

If there are no flats or sharps the key is C Major.

C Major

If there is one flat (B flat) the key is F Major.

F Major

If there is more than one flat, the key is the next to the last flat to the right. Because it is already a flat, the flat is used in the name of the key.

Eb Major   Db Major

For keys with sharps, take the last sharp to the right and go up one-half step for the name of the key.

G Major   E Major

(A key signature worksheet can be found on page 65)

Note Names Worksheet

Place the correct **treble clef** letter name in the blank under each note below.

F C C D B E G D E A

Place the correct **bass clef** letter name in the blank under each note below.

F E B D C A C F D G

Half Steps and Whole Steps Worksheet

A half step is the distance from one key to the next key (up or down) on the keyboard. A whole step skips one key. Label each of the following as a **half step** or a **whole step** in the blank below each example. You may refer to the keyboard below as needed. Be sure to watch clef signs.

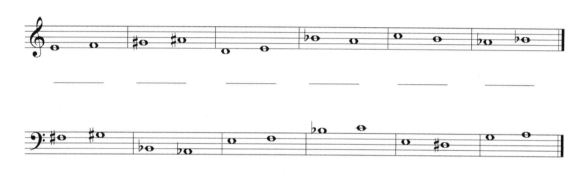

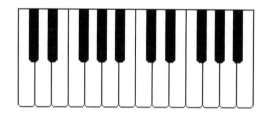

Steps and Skips Worksheet

1. A step is from one line to the space directly above or below. A skip is from a line to the next line above or below or farther apart, or from a space to the next space above or below or farther apart. A repeated note stays the same as the first note. Label the following as **steps, skips,** or **repeated** notes in the blanks below each example.

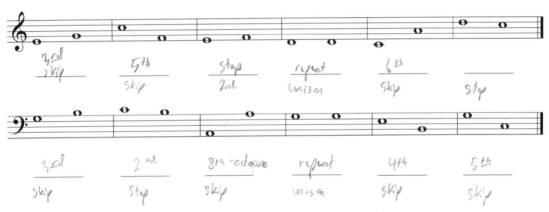

3rd
skip

5th
skip

step
2nd

repeat
unison

6th
skip

step

3rd
skip

2nd
step

8th octave
skip

repeat
unison

4th
skip

5th
skip

2. "Somer Ade" is notated below. Label each note, beginning with the second one, as a **step, skip,** or **repeated** note.

Solfege Worksheet

Write in the correct solfege name under each note in the examples below.

Bb maj

Sol Do Re Mi Re Do

A maj

Do Do Sol Sol Do Re Mi Re Ti Do

C maj

La Mi La Ti Do Ti Do La Mi

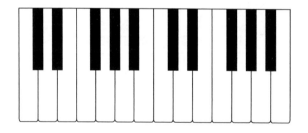

Major Scale Worksheet

Construct the following major scales. Do not change the given note. (Use accidentals rather than key signatures).

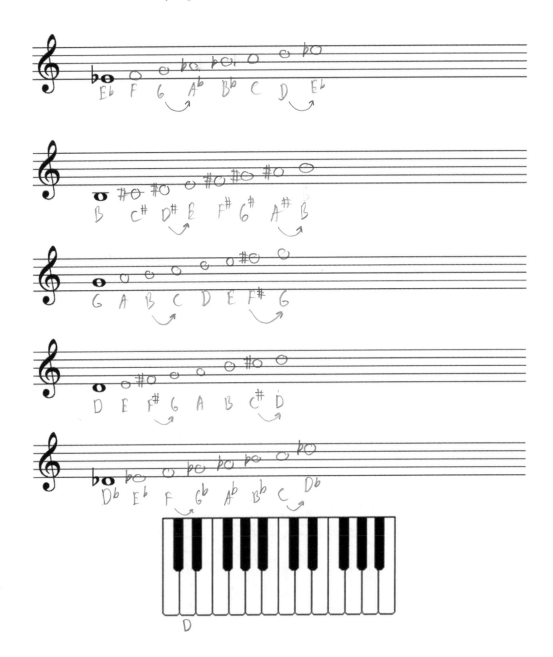

Eb F G Ab Bb C D Eb

B C# D# E F# G# A# B

G A B C D E F# G

D E F# G A B C# D

Db Eb F Gb Ab Bb C Db

D

Major Scale Worksheet #2

The first note of each scale below is correct, but each example has two or more notes that are incorrect. Change the incorrect notes to correct ones to form each major scale.

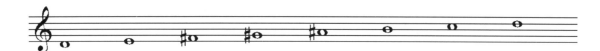

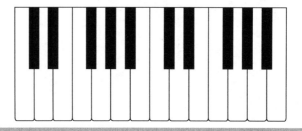

Key Signature Worksheet

Place the name of the key in the blank under each item.

"Higher than a House"

High - er than a house. High - er than a tree.

Un - der - neath the wat - er, Un - der - neath the sea. What -

ev - er can that be?

LESSON 3:1

Concept: High and Low

Objective: Students will demonstrate understanding of High and Low by placing a "star" high in the sky when a high note is heard, or placing a "starfish" low in the sea when a low note is heard.

Materials: VIDEO 3:1a and 3:1b
        Large cut out star (or smaller stars for each child)
        Visuals of high and low objects

Procedures and Strategies: Discuss things that are high (airplanes, clouds, mountain tops) and things that are low (earth worms, grass, fish in the ocean) and show visuals. Ask for examples of high things and low things in the classroom. Using a piano (or other melody instrument) demonstrate that sounds can be high or low. Play C an octave above middle C and ask the children to sing "loo" with you on this high sound. Do the same for middle C representing a low sound. Direct the children to listen for high sounds and low sounds as they watch the **VIDEO 3:1a** clip. Discuss what they heard. Especially point out the sound of the last note (on the word "be."). Watch and listen to the **VIDEO 3:1b** clip. Was the last note the same or different? Why? (If last note is high, it represents a star in the sky, if low, a starfish in the sea). Choose a child to have the teacher-made star. On high portions of song, child holds star up high, holds the star low on low portions, and at end decides whether the star will be high or low and class sings a high note or a low note. Then have all children sing song and add appropriate hand levels for high or low. Also discuss that a woman and man were heard on the song. Which one sang the high part at the beginning? (Woman) Who sang the low part in the middle of the song? (Man) Then who sang? (Both of them) How did the song end—low or high? (First time high, second time low).

"This Old Man"

This old man, he played one, he played nick - nack

on my thumb, with a nick - nack, pad - dy whack,

give a dog a bone. This old man came rol - ling home.

verse 2: on my shoe.
verse 3: on my knee.
verse 4: on my door.
verse 5: on my hive.
verse 6: on my stick.

verse 7: up in heaven.
verse 8: on the gate.
verse 9: on my spine.
verse 10: once again.

LESSON 3:2

Concept: Melodic Direction: Getting Higher

Objective: Students will correctly show the contour of "give a dog a bone" by using ascending hand levels.

Materials: VIDEO 3:2a and 3:2b
> Pictures of objects getting higher (hot air balloon rising, going up a roller coaster, an airplane taking off, etc.) and lower (sledding down a hill, going down a roller coaster, an airplane landing, etc.).
> Step bells
> Worksheet with upward, downward, and same icons

Procedures: Discuss objects getting higher or lower using pictures for motivation. Explain that a song's melody (tune) often has patterns that go higher or lower. Using step bells, which are hidden from view, play several patterns going up or going down and ask students which they heard. Bring the step bells into view and as you play patterns that are higher or lower, ask children to show the pitch rising or falling by using hand levels. View **VIDEO 3:2a,** which shows images getting higher or lower according to the contour of "This Old Man." Notice that no images are shown on "give a dog a bone." Ask students to think of that pitch pattern and determine whether it goes higher or lower. Discuss with them that the pitch was higher. As **VIDEO 3:2b** is viewed ask students to show the melody getting higher on "give a dog a bone" by using appropriate hand levels.

Assessment: With step bells hidden from view, ask selected students to play a pattern that ascends, descends, or stays the same. Students circle the appropriate icon on a worksheet.

Upward   Downward   Same

"Skin and Bones"

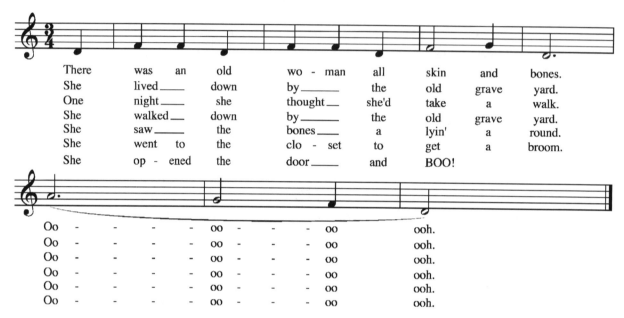

There	was	an	old	wo - man	all	skin	and	bones.
She	lived____	down	by _____	the	old	grave	yard.
One	night____	she	thought ___	she'd	take	a	walk.
She	walked__	down	by _____	the	old	grave	yard.
She	saw____	the	bones ____	a	lyin'	a	round.
She	went	to	the	clo - set	to	get	a	broom.
She	op - ened	the	door____	and	BOO!

Oo	-	-	-	-	oo	-	-	-	oo	ooh.
Oo	-	-	-	-	oo	-	-	-	oo	ooh.
Oo	-	-	-	-	oo	-	-	-	oo	ooh.
Oo	-	-	-	-	oo	-	-	-	oo	ooh.
Oo	-	-	-	-	oo	-	-	-	oo	ooh.
Oo	-	-	-	-	oo	-	-	-	oo	ooh.

LESSON 3:3

Concept: Downward pattern, expressive singing

Objective: Students will add appropriate hand and body levels to show the downward pitch pattern of the last phrase of the song. Students will communicate the mood of the song through expressive singing.

Materials: VIDEO 3:3
           Autoharp

Procedures and Strategies: View the VIDEO clip that uses images to accompany the song. Ask children how the melody moves (upward, downward, or stays the same) at the end of each verse on the "oo" portion. (Downward). Teach the song by rote. Sing the song again and have children pretend to be ghosts who "float" downward at the end of each verse.

Ask the children what they think the mood of the song is (spooky, scary, etc.) and discuss how they can make their voices match the mood. (Adding emphasis on the downbeat of each measure, sing softly until "Boo," etc.)

Assessment: As children sing the song, they show hand levels to correspond to the downward pattern of the last line of each verse. Teacher assists those having difficulty.

"Hot Dog Song"

I know a lit - tle pup - py. He has - n't an - y tail. He

is - n't ve - ry chub - by. He's skin - ny as a rail. He's

real - ly not a pup - py. He'll nev - er be a hound. They

sell him at the but - cher's store for nine - ty nine cents a pound.

Bow, wow, wow, wow, wow, wow, wow, wow. Hot Dog!

LESSON 3:4

Concepts: High and Low; Getting Higher and Lower

Objective: Students will perform the song with a "body scale" to show understanding of high and low pitches and will use hand levels to show higher and lower pitches.

Materials: VIDEO 3:4
       Eight students to form a body scale
       Step bells or song bells

Procedures and Strategies: Ask children to listen for sounds getting higher or lower as they view the VIDEO clip. Discuss that each phrase gets higher during most of the song, "Bow wows" get lower, and "Hot" is high and "Dog" is low. Teach the song by rote. Add step bells so children can see and hear when pitch ascends or descends. Then add hand levels to correspond to the pitch.

Eight children are asked to form a body scale using eight body positions that get higher:

- ♮ **1ˢᵗ child** touches toes
- ♮ **2ⁿᵈ child** touches knees
- ♮ **3ʳᵈ child** touches hips
- ♮ **4ᵗʰ child** touches waist
- ♮ **5ᵗʰ child** touches chest
- ♮ **6ᵗʰ child** touches shoulders
- ♮ **7ᵗʰ child** touches head
- ♮ **8ᵗʰ child** reaches to sky.

Another child is chosen as the "conductor." The conductor moves from one child to the next at the appropriate time as the song is sung. ("Hot Dog" can be sung at a slower tempo so the conductor can get from the highest child to the lowest). Choose eight more children for the scale, a new conductor, and continue.

Pitch Assessment: Sing the song again as entire class shows body scale positions to represent the pitch changes.

"Fleas"

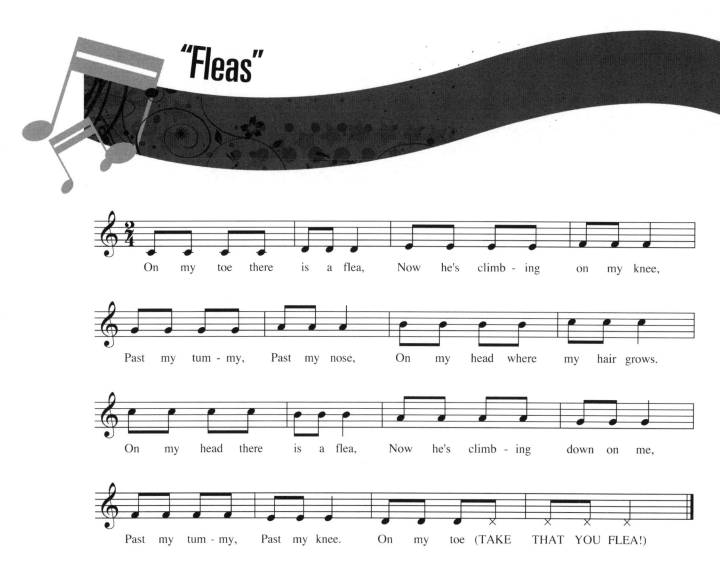

On my toe there is a flea, Now he's climb-ing on my knee,

Past my tum-my, Past my nose, On my head where my hair grows.

On my head there is a flea, Now he's climb-ing down on me,

Past my tum-my, Past my knee. On my toe (TAKE THAT YOU FLEA!)

LESSON 3:5

Concept: Higher and Lower Pitches

Objective: Students will appropriate hand levels as the pitch gets higher or lower.

Materials: VIDEO 3:5
Step bells (or song bells or piano)

Procedures and Strategies: Play the song on step bells (without singing) and ask children if the tune stays the same, gets higher, gets lower, etc. Lead them to discover that the first half is getting higher, and the second half is getting lower. Explain that the song is about fleas and discuss. View the VIDEO clip and watch as the flea climbs higher and lower. Teach the song by rote. Add motions beginning with the toe and climbing up to the head (make correlation that as notes rise our motions are getting higher), then from the head back down to the toe. Then, play the song on bells again (without singing) and ask children to show with their hands the way the pitch gets higher and then lower. When most seem to grasp the idea, add the words of the song and they can sing with the VIDEO and show hand levels.

"See Saw"

See - Saw,   up   and   down.   In   the   sky   and   on   the   ground.

LESSON 3:6

Concept: Preparation for *so, mi*

Objective: Students will stand when they hear a higher sound (*so*) and squat for a lower sound (*mi*).

Materials: VIDEO 3:6

Procedures and Strategies: Teach the song by rote. View the VIDEO clip. Ask children what they noticed about the see saw. (Sometimes a person was shown when the see saw up, sometimes when the see saw down). Make the connection that when the see saw was up, the pitch was higher, when down, the pitch was lower. Sing along with the VIDEO clip. Children stand and form a circle, as song is repeated they stand for every higher sound in the song and squat for each lower sound.

Game: Children are in pairs, facing their partner. Children stand for higher pitches and squat for lower pitches. Variation: Pair joins raised right arms. Arm remains raised for high sounds, lowered for low sounds.

Extension: Add an ostinato with the song, sung by a few children: First they sing Up, Down and then *so, mi* to the beat.

"Star Light"

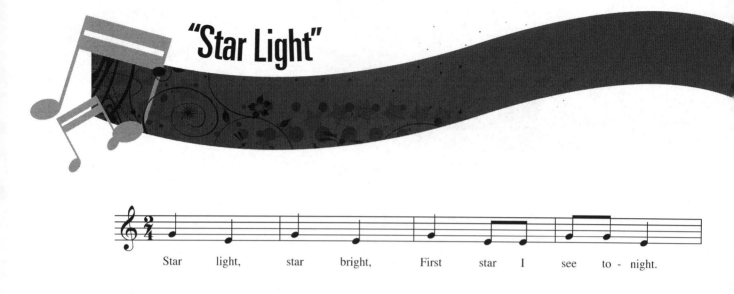

Star light, star bright, First star I see to-night.

Wish I may, wish I might, Have the wish I wish to-night.

LESSON 3:7

Concept: *so* and *mi*

Objective: Students will label higher sounds *so* and lower sounds *mi* and will sing *so* for higher sounds and *mi* for lower sounds in place of the text.

Materials: VIDEO 3:7a and **3:7b**
    Board for song "notation"
    23 star shapes

Procedures and Strategies: Teach the song by rote. Ask students to notice that some stars are higher, some are lower as the **VIDEO 3:7a** clip is shown. Play the clip again and children stand when they hear a higher sound, squat for a lower sound. Repeat clip and children use hand levels to represent higher or lower pitches. "Notate" song on board by placing stars, higher or lower, to represent each pitch. Tell the children that the higher star has a special name, "*so*" and the lower star is named "*mi*." Solicit volunteers to come forward and write S or M in each star. When completed, sing the song with *so* and *mi* instead of the words. Repeat while viewing **VIDEO 3:7b,** which has each star labeled as S or M.

"The Counting Song"

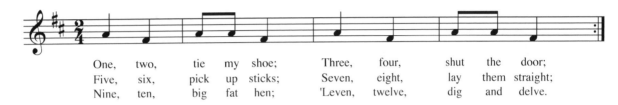

One,	two,	tie	my	shoe;	Three,	four,	shut	the	door;
Five,	six,	pick	up	sticks;	Seven,	eight,	lay	them	straight;
Nine,	ten,	big	fat	hen;	'Leven,	twelve,	dig	and	delve.

LESSON 3:8

Concept: *so* and *mi*

Objective: Students will use hand levels for *so* and *mi* and substitute *so* and *mi* for the text.

Materials: VIDEO 3:8a and **VIDEO 3:8b**
Board to show partial staff (2 lines)

Procedures and Strategies: Teach the song by rote. View the **VIDEO 3:8a** clip and ask children to notice that the images are high or low, corresponding to the tune. Repeat the clip and ask children to use hand levels to show the higher and lower pitches. (Remind them that the higher pitch is *so* and the lower one *mi*). Also discuss the fact that music can be shown by using lines and spaces to show higher or lower notes and illustrate on board explaining that if *so* is on the top line, *mi* is on the bottom line. (The VIDEO uses a 2-line partial staff. View the clip again, this time with the volume turned down and children singing *so* and *mi* instead of the words.

Then view **VIDEO 3:8b** (with volume back on). Ask children to sing *so* and *mi* again noting that solfege syllables are shown on the VIDEO clip.

"Clap Your Hands"

Clap,   clap,   clap your hands,   Clap your hands to - geth - er.
Stamp,   stamp,   stamp your feet,   Stamp your feet to - geth - er.

LESSON 3:9   Version Two of "Clap Your Hands"

Concepts: Introduction of partial staff; *so* and *mi* hand signs introduced; *ta* and *ti ti* review

Objectives: Students will label notes as *so* and *mi* on a partial staff and will create patterns which use *so* and *mi* and *ta* and *ti ti*. Students will use Curwen hand signs for *so* and *mi* as they sing "Clap Your Hands."

Materials: VIDEO 3:9a and VIDEO 3:9b
Board with 2-line staves drawn
Paper with a two-line staff for each student

Procedures and Strategies: Review the song, "Clap Your Hands." View **VIDEO 3:9a** and review partial staff and that *so* is represented by higher notes, those on the top line, and *mi* is shown on the lower line. Point out that in music, when we say a note is on a line, that the line goes right through the middle of the note. (This is different than in printing when the teacher tells them to print letters on the line!). The teacher copies the song (on a two-line staff) as the class echoes the tune singing *so* or *mi* as the teacher places notes on the partial staff. Remind the children that the note lengths will be shorter when *ti ti* is used because there are two sounds to the beat and longer when the notes are *ta*.

Explain that we can "play a game" using different hand positions to represent different notes or syllables. For *so* we use a vertical hand with the thumb pointing up and for *mi* we use a horizontal hand. Ask whether *so* or *mi* hand position should be higher. (*So* should be higher because it is a higher pitch). Demonstrate and have children imitate. Practice *so* and *mi* echo patterns where the teacher does a three or four beat pattern using hand signs and the class echoes. Then view **VIDEO 3:9b** where hand signs are shown for the tune.

Assessment: Distribute paper to each child with a two-line partial staff. Ask children to compose a four beat pattern, which uses *so* and *mi* and *ta* and at least one group of *ti ti*'s. Teacher circulates and evaluates children's work. Volunteers sing their tune (with *so* or *mi*) or clap the rhythm (*ta* or *ti ti*) and the class echoes.

"Rain, Rain"

Rain,   Rain,   go   a - way;   Come   a - gain   some   oth - er   day.
Sun - shine's   here   to   stay,   Now   we   can   go   out to   play.

LESSON 3:10

Concept: Introduction of *la*; Review of *so* and *mi*

Objective: Students will place hands on waist for *so*, hands on knees for *mi*, and hands on shoulders for *la* when *so, mi, la* patterns are heard. Students will repeat *so, mi, la* patterns with solfege and correct Curwen hand signs.

Materials: VIDEO 3:10a and **3:10b**
          Song bells

Procedures and Strategies: Ask students to raise their hand on any pitch other than *so* or *mi* as the song is taught by rote. Check that they identify the pitch on the word "some." Show **VIDEO 3:10a** and reinforce that the image shown on the word "some" is higher. This new note is called **la**. Sing the song again, and for each *so*, children place hands on waist, for each *mi* place hands on knees, and for *La* place hands on shoulders.

Game: Play the *so, mi, la* game. First the teacher sings a series of patterns using *so, mi,* and *la* and the class echoes. Show the hand sign for *la* (a cupped position with fingers pointing down). Now sing and sign *so, mi, la* patterns and children echo by singing and using hand signs.

When the children seem secure, begin signing one note in the pattern, but not singing it. Children still sing and sign all of the notes. Conversely, you can sing and not sign, but children still do both. Eventually, play *so, mi, la* patterns on song bells (situated where children cannot see them) and children sing and sign the patterns played. Children really enjoy this. Make sure you provide a mixture of repetition and challenge and play the game often!

Extension: After the above game is played, have the children sing "Rain, Rain" with hand signs. When ready, view **VIDEO 3:10b** that shows the hand signs and have children sing and sign along.

"Lucy Locket"

Luc - y Lock - et   lost her pock - et,   Kit - ty Fish - er   found it,
Not a pen - ny   was there in it,   on - ly rib - bon   round it.

LESSON 3:11

Concept: *so, mi, la; piano* and *forte* discrimination

Objective: Students will accurately sing *so, mi,* and *la* patterns and show correct Curwen hand signs to accompany tonal patterns.

Materials: VIDEO 3:11

Procedures: View VIDEO clip and ask children how many different levels were used for the "pocket" or purse. (Three) Why? (Because the song has three pitches: *so, mi, la*). Review that *la* is highest, *so* is in the middle, and *mi* is the lowest note. Review hand signs for *S, M, L* and sing and sign patterns for children to echo.

Extension: Play the following game for *piano* (soft) and *forte* (loud) discrimination.

Game directions: The teacher holds a "pocket" or purse. One child is chosen to hide the pocket, another child to find it. (Instructions can be given to hide it on top of an object, under an object, beside an object, etc.) Teacher covers the finder's eyes and creates various sound effects while the hider is hiding the pocket. The hider returns to the teacher and says ready when it has been hidden. Children begin singing the song, at a soft dynamic level when the finder is far from the pocket, and gradually louder as the finder nears the pocket. When the pocket is found, children finish the song by clapping the steady beat and singing loudly until the finder returns the pocket to the teacher.

"Snail, Snail"

Snail, Snail, Snail, Snail, Go a - round and round and round.

LESSON 3:12

Concepts: *so, mi,* and *la* and Inner Hearing

Objective: Students will sing *so, mi,* and *la* patterns and add the correct hand signs to the song. Students will demonstrate inner hearing competence by alternately singing a portion of the song and "hearing" a portion of the song that is not sung.

Materials: VIDEO 3:12a and **VIDEO 3:12V**
       Chalkboard
       Snail puppet

Procedures and Strategies: Teach the song by rote. View **VIDEO 3:12a** that shows snails at three levels on a two-line staff and lead children to derive the hand signs (*S, M, L*) and notate on board. Sing again with solfege and hand signs.

View **VIDEO 3:12V,** which shows children playing an inner hearing game. Using a snail puppet, try the activity with the children. Explain to the children that when the snail's head is out, they should sing out. When the snail's head is in, they continue singing inside their head. When the snail's head comes back out, they join in singing the song at the appropriate place. (Kodály refers to this as "inner hearing.")

"Doggie, Doggie"

Dog - gie, Dog - gie, Where's your bone? Some - one took it from my home.

Who has the - bone?_____ I have the - bone._____

LESSON 3:13

Concept: *so, mi, la*; tone matching

Objective: Students will attempt to match pitches of *so*, *mi*, and *la* by singing solos to a question/answer song.

Materials: VIDEO 3:13V
>Song bells
>Dog puppet
>Clave or rawhide bone

Procedures and Strategies: Review *so, mi, la* patterns by singing them, signing them, and playing patterns on song bells for children to repeat. Teach "Doggie, Doggie" by rote and view VIDEO of children playing a game. Then have class try the game using props.

Game Directions: The entire class sings the first phrase ("Doggie, Doggie where's your bone?") and the third phrase ("Who stole the bone?") of the song. Two children are chosen to sing the solo answers to the questions. One child has a dog puppet and sings the second phrase. The other child has a clave (bone) and sings the fourth phrase. The "doggie" chooses a different child and the "bone" chooses a different child.

Assessment: This game is an excellent opportunity for children to become comfortable with singing alone. The game and manipulatives make it fun.

The teacher should listen carefully to each child and encourage those who have difficulty matching the pitch to listen carefully to the tune, try it again, etc. Be positive, but unless you let the child know the tune isn't correct, they may never know they are having trouble matching pitch. Helpful hints: use hand levels to show pitch changes, sing with them, match the tone that they are singing so they can hear the difference, and persevere!

"Bounce High, Bounce Low"

Bounce high, Bounce low, Bounce the ball to Shi - loh.

LESSON 3:14

Concept: *so, mi, la* on partial staff

Objective: Students will create patterns using *so, mi,* and *la* on a 2-line staff and will sing and sign *so, mi, la* from their "compositions."

Materials: VIDEO 3:14a and 3:14b
Teacher-made felt boards with 2 lines and felt circles for placing *so, la* and *mi*. (or paper with 2 staff lines drawn)

Procedures and Strategies: Teach the song by rote. View **VIDEO 3:14a** of song that shows balls at different heights to represent *so, mi,* or *la*. Review placement of *so* and *mi* on a two-line staff and explain that if *so* is on a line, *la* is shown above the line. View **VIDEO 3:14b** that features a two-line staff superimposed over the images, and ask children to sing and sign the solfege. Distribute felt boards and ask children to "compose" a four- or eight- beat pattern using *so, mi,* and *la*. (Place felt circles at appropriate places). Solicit volunteers to show their work and ask class to sing and sign the solfege.

"Bye Baby Bunting"

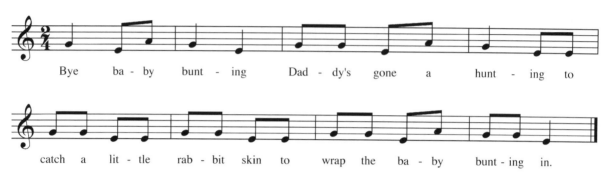

Bye ba - by bunt - ing Dad - dy's gone a hunt - ing to

catch a lit - tle rab - bit skin to wrap the ba - by bunt - ing in.

LESSON 3:15   Version Two of "Bye Baby Bunting"

Concept: *so, mi, la* on a partial staff

Objective: Students will determine solfege (*so, mi* or *la*) from a two-line staff.

Materials: VIDEO 3:15
Chalkboard

Procedures and Strategies: Review the song with the children. View the VIDEO clip that has the song notated on a two-line staff without *so, mi,* or *la* written below the staff. Sing through the song with solfege and hand signs.

Extension: Teacher writes partial staff notation of the song on board, one measure at a time, and asks volunteers to sing the pattern using correct pitch, rhythm, and solfege.

"Wee Willie Winkie"

Wee Wil - lie Win - kie runs through the town,
f

Up - stairs and down - stairs in his night gown.
p

Rap - ping at the win - dow, cry - ing through the lock,
f

Are the child - ren in their beds? For it's eight o' - clock.
p

LESSON 3:16

Concepts: Moveable *do*; *piano* and *forte* discrimination

Objective: Students will demonstrate understanding of moveable *do* by completing solfege (*so, mi, la*) of "Wee Willie Winkie" in two different keys. Students will sing loudly when score indicates *forte* and softly when score indicates *piano*.

Materials: VIDEO 3:16a, 3:16b, and 3:16c
        Chalkboard

Procedures and Strategies: Teach the song by rote. Then view **VIDEO 3:16a** which shows song notated with two staff lines in the key of C. Point out that *so* is on the top line, *mi* is on the bottom line, and *la* is above the top line. (In a space). Notice that only the 1st and 3rd phrases are notated. Sing the song again and ask children to think about how the 2nd and 4th phrases would be notated. Discuss and write correct answers on board. View **VIDEO 3:16b** that has the entire song notated.

View **VIDEO 3:16c** and ask what is different. Now *so* is in a space, *mi* is in the space below, and *la* is on the top line. Explain that *S, M,* and *L* move if we sing a tune in a higher pitch or in a lower pitch. However, because each note moves the same distance, the tune is still recognizable. This idea is known as "Moveable *do*." Sing the solfege with hand signs in this new key.

Ask children to suggest songs they know and sing them in different keys to help them realize that the tune is still recognizable even though the song is higher or lower.

Point out the *f* and *p* in the music. Explain that *f* stands *forte*, which means loud in Italian, and that *p* stands for *piano*, meaning soft. Sing "Wee Willie Winkie" observing the dynamic marks. Experiment with other songs, loud and soft, and see what songs seem as though they should be sung loudly or softly. What contributes to this feeling? (Mood, tempo, etc.)

LESSON 3:17

Concept: *do, re, mi, so* song (preparation for pentatonic scale)

Objective: Students will correctly identify *do, re, mi* and *so* and sing those solfege syllables using correct hand signs.

Materials: VIDEO 3:17a, 3:17b, and **3:17c**
        "Hot Cross Buns" song
        Chalkboard
        Paper with three-staff lines

Procedures and Strategies: Use the whole song method to teach the song. View **VIDEO 3:17a** that shows a squirrel at four different levels, corresponding to four notes of the scale. Introduce *do* and *re* and their respective hand signs. Use board to show relationship of *do* and *re* to *mi*. Ask children if they can think of any song they know that uses *do, re,* and *mi.* ("Hot Cross Buns"). Sing "Hot Cross Buns" with words first and then with solfege and hand signs and have students repeat.

Review *do, re, mi,* and *so* by signing and singing patterns and have the students repeat. View **VIDEO 3:17b** that shows the notes *do, re, mi* and *so* labeled on a three-line staff as "Let Us Chase the Squirrel" is sung. Ask children first to sing using solfege, and then using solfege and hand signs. View **VIDEO 3:17c** that has the hand signs shown as the song is sung.

Assessment: Distribute three-line staff paper and ask students to create a measure or two using *do, re, mi* and *so.* Circulate to check results.

"Great Big House in New Orleans"

Great big house in New Or - leans, for - ty sto - ries high ____:

Ev' - ry room that I been in, filled with pump - kin pie.

2. Went down to the old mill stream to fetch a pail of water;
   Put one arm around my wife, the other round my daughter.

3. Fare thee well, my darling girl, fare thee well, my daughter;
   Fare thee well, my darling girl, with the golden slippers on her.

LESSON 3:18

Concept: Pentatonic scale

Objective: Students will accurately label solfege and sing solfege with hand signs to "Great Big House."

Materials: VIDEO 3:18a and 3:18b
Space for movement

Procedures and Strategies: Discuss with students that a pentagon has five sides. In music we refer to a scale having five tones as being a "pentatonic" scale. Unlike a major scale (*do, re, mi, fa, so, la, ti, do*) a pentatonic scale has no half steps. *Fa* and *ti* are omitted and the pentatonic scale uses the remaining five syllables: *do, re, mi, so,* and *la.* Sing up and down the pentatonic scale with solfege and demonstrate the Curwen hand signs. Ask students to repeat. Sing and sign various pentatonic patterns and have students repeat. View **VIDEO 3:18a,** which shows the notation of "Great Big House" on a partial staff. Have students to sign (without singing) while watching the clip. Then view **VIDEO 3:18b,** which shows the hand signs being performed as the song is sung. Students can sing and sign while viewing the clip.

Game: "Great Big House" is an Appalachian folk song, which was accompanied by a dulcimer and dancing. Teach the students the following movement:

Formation: Single circle of partners, standing. (Choose partners by counting by 2's around the circle)

Movement:

🎼 **Verse 1**: All join hands and circle to the left with a strutting step for 8 counts and then turn and strut to the right for 8 counts.

🎼 **Verse 2**: All drop hands. "Ones" take 4 steps toward the center of the circle, join hands, and simulate picking up a pail of water (dip and rise). "Twos" tap foot on beat, alternating with clapping hands, for eight beats. On "Put one arm around my wife" take four steps in, join hands, and put joined hands over top of "ones" heads. On "the other 'round my daughter" everyone backs up four steps making a "basket-weave."

🎼 **Verse 3**: "Ones" swing the "two" on their right by joining left arms, twice around. (8 counts). "Ones" swing the "two" on their left by joining right arms, twice around. (8 counts).

"Hello There!"

Hel - lo there! (Hel - lo there!) How are you? (How are you?) It's

so good (It's so good) To see you. (To see you.) We'll

sing and (We'll sing and) be hap - py (be hap - py) That we're

all here to geth - er a - gain.

LESSON 3:19

Concept: Pitch Matching

Objective: Students will match pitch by echoing phrases sung by the teacher and by singing the song in pairs, echoing each other with a reasonable degree of accuracy.

Materials: VIDEO 3:19V
Autoharp

Procedures and Strategies: This is an excellent warm-up song for the start of each class period. View **VIDEO 3:19V** of children echoing teacher and then teacher echoing the children. Teach the song and sing with the video. Review the song without the video and accompany on autoharp. Then, boys sing the melody, girls echo; or those wearing blue sing the melody, those wearing red echo, etc.

Assessment: To assess **steady beat** ability of students, have a child play steady strums on the autoharp to accompany the song. (Teacher presses the correct buttons). To assess the ability to **match pitch**, have children take turns singing the songs in pairs, one child sings the melody, the other the echo. Or, class sings the melody, and one child sings the echo.

"Scotland's Burning"

Scot - land's burn - ing, Scot - land's burn - ing, Look out! Look out!

Fire! Fire! Fire! Fire! Pour on wa - ter, pour on wa - ter!

LESSON 3:20

Concept: Steps and Skips

Objective: Students will correctly label each note of the song as a repeated note, a step, or a skip.

Materials: VIDEO 3:20
Chalkboard for song notation
Step bells

Procedures and Strategies: Teach the song by rote. Using the step bells, ask for a volunteer to demonstrate playing by step—playing each bell upward or downward. Ask another student to demonstrate how you might play a skip (skip at least one note between two played notes). Explain, using staff notation on the board, that a **step** is from one line on the staff to a space above or below or from one space to a line above or below. Show that a **skip** is from a line to a line or farther apart or from a space to a space or farther apart on the staff. Demonstrate that a **repeated** note simply means that the same note occurs again.

View the VIDEO clip that shows the notation of "Scotland's Burning." Ask students to identify each repeated note, step, or skip throughout the song.

Assessment: Ask students to copy the notation of "Scotland's Burning" and to indicate under each note if it represents a repeated note, a step, or a skip from the previous note.

"St. Paul's Steeple"

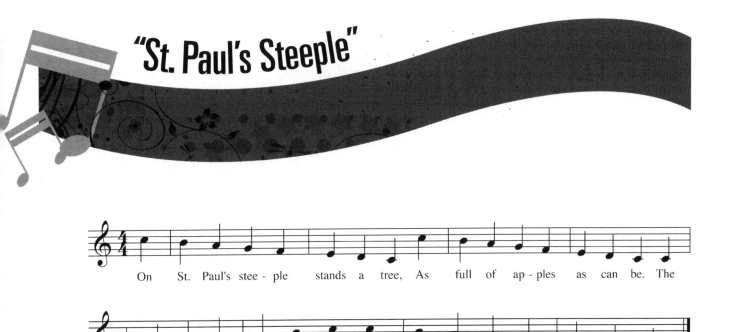

On St. Paul's stee-ple stands a tree, As full of ap-ples as can be. The

lit-tle boys of Lon-don town, They run with hooks to pull them down.

LESSON 3:21

Concept: Major scale

Objective: Students will correctly order the eight pitches of a major scale from high to low and will use correct hand signs and solfege while singing the tune.

Materials: **VIDEO 3:21a** and **3:21b**
  Step bells
  Boom whackers or resonator bells for C Major scale.

Procedures and Strategies: Teach the song by rote. While the children sing the song again, play the song on step bells and ask them what they noticed about the pitch. (It went down by step on each phrase, except the third, which went up by step). Explain that each phrase represents the **major scale** either going upwards or downwards. Play the scale going up and down without the song so students can hear the scale pattern. View **VIDEO 3:21a** that shows the notation of each phrase.

Choose eight children and randomly distribute the eight boom whacker tubes or the resonator bells. Ask them to line up facing the class and to play their note when you point to them during the song. Stop after the first or second phrase and ask the class if the notes played sounded like the major scale. (They should notice that it did not match the scale). Ask the instrumentalists to play again without the class singing to ensure that everyone hears that it doesn't sound like a correct scale.

Ask how you can "fix" the problem so that it sounds like a correct scale? Then have two students play, one after the other and rearrange the children so that they form a correct scale from high to low.

View the **VIDEO 3:21a** clip again and ask children to show the pitch level with their hands as they sing. Introduce *fa* and *ti* and the accompanying Curwen hand signs. Practice singing up and down the scale using solfege and hand signs. View **VIDEO 3:21b,** which shows hand signs as the song is sung.

"Teddy Bear"

Ted-dy Bear, Ted-dy Bear, turn a - round   Ted-dy Bear, Ted-dy Bear,   touch the ground.

Ted-dy Bear, Ted-dy Bear, switch off the light,   Ted-dy Bear, Ted-dy Bear, say "Good night."

LESSON 3:22

Concept: Pentatonic scale

Objective: Students accurately label the notes of "Teddy Bear" as *do, re, mi, so,* or *la* and will sing the song with solfege and hand signs.

Materials: VIDEO 3:22V
Chalkboard

Procedures and Strategies: Teach the song by rote. View VIDEO video clip of students singing the song with movements corresponding to what the text describes. Ask students to listen to the pitch on the words "Teddy Bear, Teddy Bear" as you sing the song again. Lead them to understand that each time "Teddy Bear, Teddy Bear" was sung, the tune was so so mi, so so mi. Is the tune the same or different on "turn around?" Notate that measure on a three-line staff and ask for a volunteer to write in the solfege. Continue until entire song is notated. Discuss that the song is pentatonic (5 tone) because it uses *do, re, mi, so,* and *la.* Ask the class to sing the song with you using hand signs and solfege instead of the words.

Interval Worksheet

An interval is determined by counting the line or space of the bottom note and each line or space up to and including the line or space of the top note. Place the correct number for each interval in the blank below each example.

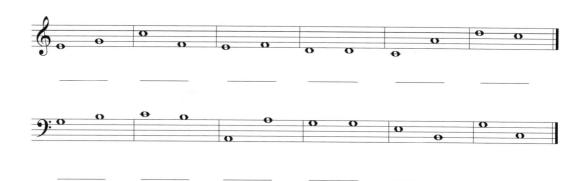

Harmony and Texture

Harmony occurs when two or more notes are sung or played simultaneously. Although much emphasis is given to singing in unison in the elementary grades, children also need to become aware of harmony and its functions in music. The earliest recognition of harmony often comes from an *accompaniment* to a song. Accompaniments create harmony because they contain notes other than those of the melody. Music teachers often choose to accompany songs on autoharp, guitar, or piano. Simple accompaniments can also be played on Orff instruments or other melody instruments. To heighten awareness of harmony, the accompaniment can be played without singing while children are asked to listen to the difference between the melody and the harmony.

Adding an *ostinato* or short, repeated pattern to be sung or played with the melody is another way for students to experience harmony. The last phrase of "Are You Sleeping" can be used as an ostinato throughout the song. After the entire class rehearses the ostinato, "Ding, Ding, Dong. Ding, Ding, Dong," select a few students to sing the ostinato while the remainder of the class sings the melody. The ostinato can also be played on song bells or Orff instruments.

Are you sleep-ing? Are you sleep-ing? Bro-ther John, Bro-ther John,

Morn-ing bells are ring-ing, Morn-ing bells are ring-ing, Ding, Ding, Dong, Ding, Ding, Dong.

Ostinato:

Ding, Ding, Dong.   Ding, Ding, Dong.

(See activity 4:1a and 4:1b in the book and accompanying video clips).

Rounds can also be used to teach harmony. A *round* occurs when two or more groups sing the melody of a song, but enter at different times. Harmony results because the groups are singing different segments of the melody at the same time. Many songs cannot be sung as rounds. A round needs to have phrases that sound pleasing, or harmonious, when sung together. Songbooks and textbooks will indicate that a song can be sung as a round by inserting Roman numerals in the text where additional parts can begin or by labeling the song as a round. Some students tend to cover their ears during initial experiences in singing rounds. Teachers need to discourage that because the idea is for children to hear both parts. With ears covered it is difficult for students to hear their own part, let alone the harmony parts. One of the most familiar rounds for American children is "Row, Row, Row Your Boat" which is notated below. Notice the Roman numerals that indicate when different groups can begin singing.

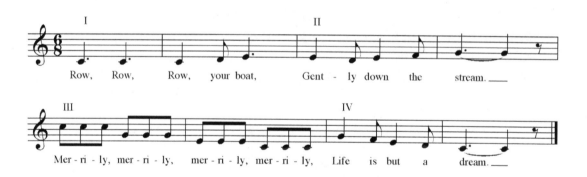

Row,   Row,   Row,   your boat,   Gent - ly down   the   stream. ___

Mer - ri - ly, mer - ri - ly,   mer - ri - ly, mer - ri - ly,   Life   is but   a   dream. ___

Partner songs also create harmony. *Partner songs* are two songs that can be sung simultaneously because they have similar structure and chord patterns. Partner songs need to be sung in the same key. Common partner songs include:

"Bow Belinda" with "Skip to My Lou,"
"Home on the Range" with "My Home's in Montana,"
"Go Tell Aunt Rhody" with "London Bridge," and
"Sally Go 'Round the Sun" with "Looby Lou."

"Row, Row, Row, Your Boat" notated above, works as a partner song with "The Farmer in the Dell" notated below. Compare and contrast the melodies and try singing them as partner songs in class or with a partner.

Descants, added harmony parts usually written higher than a melody, also offer a chance for harmonic exploration. Students might have heard descants by church choirs when the sopranos sing a higher melody on the last verse of a hymn.

After students can successfully sing rounds and partner songs, two-part singing can be introduced. *Two-part singing* takes place when two independent parts, Soprano and Alto, are sung at the same time. Students in fifth and sixth grade should be given many opportunities for two-part singing. Both boys and girls can generally sing alto or soprano until the voice change takes place. When introducing two-part singing, have the entire class sing each part until they are familiar with it and then divide into Soprano and Alto groups. "America" provides a good beginning example for two-part singing because both parts begin and end on the same note (unison).

(See "The Three Rogues" activity 4:2 and accompanying video clip for an example of a descant).

America

In the upper elementary grades, many activities related to harmony involve chords. A *chord* is made up of at least three notes played or sung simultaneously. When a chord has three notes, built in intervals of a third for each note, it is called a *triad*. The "Western" music tradition, which includes American music, gives prominence to three triads known as the *primary chords*. The primary chords are built on the first, fourth, and fifth notes of the scale. Triads are identified in three distinct ways:

1. Shown with an upper case Roman numeral if a major triad, or a lower case Roman numeral if a minor chord.
2. Identified with the letter name of the *root*, or bottom note, of the chord. An upper case letter signifies a major triad while a lower case letter indicates the chord is a minor triad.
3. Each note of the scale is given a name to identify the chord built on that scale degree. *Tonic* refers to the triad built on the first note, *Subdominant* refers to the triad built on the fourth note, and *Dominant* refers to the triad built on the fifth note of the scale.

The chart below shows the primary chords in the key of C labeled in the above ways. The names associated with the triads built on other scale degrees (notes) are shown above the staff.

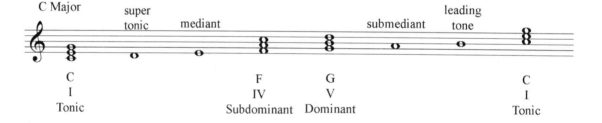

The letter names of the chords will change from one key to the next, but Tonic (I), Subdominant (IV), and Dominant (V) are still built on the first, fourth, and fifth scale degrees of the new key. Therefore, in the Key of F Major, shown below, the I chord (Tonic) is now built on F rather than on C as it was in C Major.

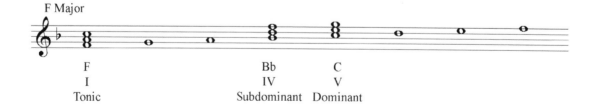

(See Triad Worksheet on page 105 and Chord activities 4.2 and accompanying video.)

If a note is a sharp or flat in a scale, the flat or sharp is used when constructing triads. For example, in the key of B flat Major, the IV chord would be built on E flat with the other notes being G (natural) and B flat. The scale and key signature contain B flat and E flat which mean that all B's and E's are flats. A *major triad* is constructed by using a root of the chord on the bottom, a note two whole steps higher (4 half steps) in the middle, and a note one and a half steps higher (3 half steps) on the top.

Texture

The term *texture* in music can be used in a variety of ways. We sometimes refer to thin (a few notes at once) or thick texture (many notes at once), or to light (few instruments/ softer instruments) or heavy texture (many instruments/louder instruments). However, most often texture refers to the interplay of melody and harmony. A melody heard without accompaniment is referred to as *monophonic*, meaning one sound. Children singing a song in unison, and Gregorian chant are examples of monophonic music. Monophonic music can be illustrated with the icon below representing the melody.

Sing "Are You Sleeping" unaccompanied, in unison to hear an example of monophonic texture.

A melody with an accompaniment is referred to as *homophonic*, meaning same sound. The melody is accompanied with chord tones. Examples of homophonic music include hymns and most popular songs. Homophonic texture can be represented with chord tones shown below the melody line.

Sing "Are You Sleeping" with autoharp or guitar accompaniment to hear an example of homophonic texture.

Another type of texture is *polyphonic*, meaning many sounds. There are two types of polyphony: a melody that is imitated, or two or more different melodies played together. J. S. Bach was a master of polyphonic music and composed both types. A round is an example of polyphony in which a melody is imitated. A single melody line occurring at different intervals can represent a melody that is imitated.

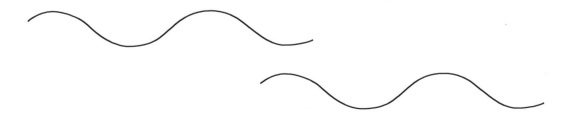

Sing "Are You Sleeping" as a round, unaccompanied, to hear an example of polyphonic texture.

The second type of polyphony can be represented by two different shapes to illustrate that the melodies are not the same.

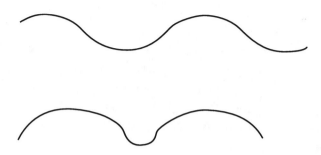

A final type of texture is referred to as ***mixed texture***. Mixed texture is a combination of either type of polyphony with chordal accompaniment. An iconic representation for mixed texture appears below.

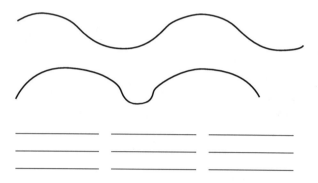

Sing "Are You Sleeping" as a round with autoharp or guitar accompaniment to hear an example of mixed texture.

Chord Worksheets

1. Complete a **Major** scale starting on the given note. Construct and appropriately label the primary chords (I, IV, and V). Remember to add all needed sharps or flats in the scale and chords.

G Major

Db Major

2. If the triads below are major triads, label them with the correct letter name of the chord. If they are not major chords change the middle note by raising it one-half step so that it becomes a major chord and label it with the correct letter name as well. (Major triads have two whole steps between the root and middle notes and a step and a half between the top two notes).

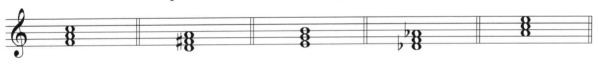

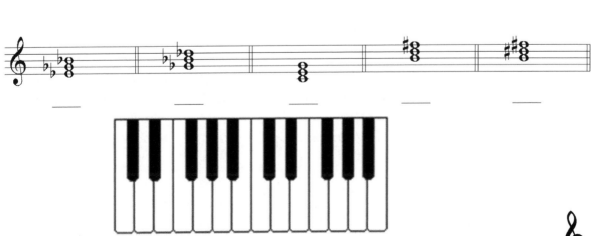

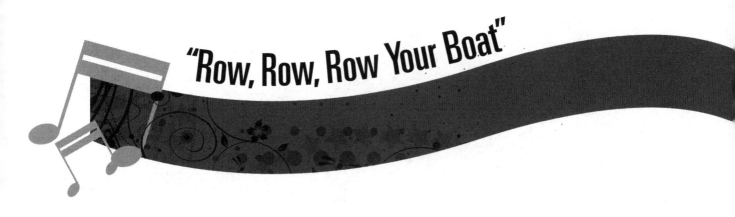

"Row, Row, Row Your Boat"

Row, Row, Row, your boat, Gent - ly down the stream. ____

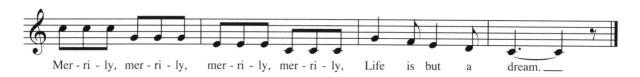

Mer - ri - ly, mer - ri - ly, mer - ri - ly, mer - ri - ly, Life is but a dream. ____

LESSON 4:1

Concepts: Rhythmic canon and melodic canon

Objective: Students will perform a rhythmic canon of patterns clapped by the teacher. Students will sing "Row, Row, Row Your Boat" in a 2-part canon.

Materials: **Video Clips 4:1a** and **4:1b**

Procedures and Strategies: Teacher claps rhythmic patterns and children echo (4 beats at a time). Then, using only *ta* and *ti ti* patterns, ask the children to echo what you are clapping, four beats after you without pausing in between. Begin with an 8 beat pattern, and extend the length as children are able. Remind them that they have to watch you closely in order to be successful. Tell them that what they just performed was a canon. A canon occurs when one group imitates the same pattern, but begins at a different time.

Canons can also occur in the melody, or tune of a song. Ask children how that would work. (Two groups sing the same tune, but start at different times). Teach "Row, Row" by rote. View the **4:1a** clip that shows a rowboat with the tune of the song. Then view the **4:1b** clip which shows a 2nd rowboat when the tune of the canon (or round) would start. Then teacher sings song and directs when children come in to create the canon. Divide the class and perform canon again. Solicit two volunteers to sing it as a canon (teacher joins in on either part as needed).

Extension: Explain that a round or canon creates ***polyphony***. Polyphony, meaning "many sounds," results when another group (or groups0 enters at different times imitating the song. A second type of polyphony occurs when there are two independent or different melodies occurring at the same time. Many compositions by J. S. Bach, a Baroque composer, illustrate polyphony.

"The Three Rogues"

LESSON 4:2

Concept: Harmony: Group singing and solo singing with a descant

Objective: Selected students will sing the melody of "The Three Rogues" as a solo, while being accompanied by a descant.

Materials: Video Clips 4:2

Procedures and Strategies: Play Video 4:2 and ask students whether they heard a melody alone, or a melody with an added harmonic part. Explain that the added part is known as a ***descant***. Teach the melody by rote until the students can sing it securely. Then ask students to sing the melody while you sing the descant. Repeat as needed. Then teach students the descant part. Ask half of the class to sing the melody and half the descant. Solicit volunteers to sing the melody as a solo (without descant). Add descant with solos as children ready. (This will not occur in a single class period, but can be a source of tremendous accomplishment for the children when they can maintain the melody part as a solo).

"America"

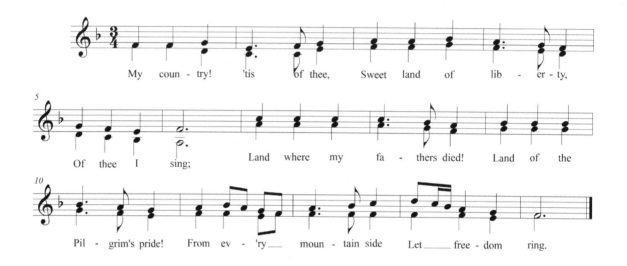

My coun - try! 'tis of thee, Sweet land of lib - er - ty,

Of thee I sing; Land where my fa - thers died! Land of the

Pil - grim's pride! From ev - 'ry moun - tain side Let free - dom ring.

LESSON 4.3

Concepts: Harmony, Two-part singing, Intervals

Objective: Students will accurately sing the soprano and alto parts of "America" and will correctly identify intervals formed by the soprano and alto parts.

Materials: Two-part notated version of "America" for each student
        Piano

Procedures and Strategies: Ask class to sing the melody of "America" with you. Show the music and ask why there are two notes shown for almost all syllables of the text. (The top note indicates the soprano part and the bottom note indicates the alto part.) Point out that when the soprano and alto part has the same note there is a stem going up and a stem going down for that note. Discuss vocal ranges of sopranos, altos, tenors, and basses and that the tenor and bass line are written in bass clef because they sing in a lower register. Play the soprano and alto parts together on the piano as the class listens. Sing the alto part alone and then have the class sing the alto part with you. Then divide class and half sing the soprano and half sing the alto. Switch parts. Ask for volunteers to sing a duet with one on a part (or two or three on a part if they are not yet comfortable singing a duet.)

Extension: Distribute copies of the two-part notated version of "America." Review that an intervals is the distance from one note to the next and that harmonic or vertical intervals are counted by numbering the line or space of the bottom note, each line and space between the notes, and the line or space of the top note. Ask students to label each interval formed by the alto and soprano lines.

You may wish to do the first couple of intervals together as a class. Review students' answers when they have finished.

Joe Turner Blues

American Blues

1.They tell me___ Joe Turn-er's___ come and gone.___
2.He came here___ with for-ty___ links of chain.___
3.Joe Turn-er,___ he took my___ man a-way.___

They tell me___ Joe Turn-er's___ come and gone.___
He came here___ with for-ty___ links of chain.___
Joe Turn-er,___ he took my___ man a-way.___

He left me ___ here to sing ___ this ___ song.

LESSON 4:4

Concept: Primary chords and 12-bar blues Form

Objective: Students will determine the correct notes for the C, F, and G7 chords and play a correct chord tone on the beat to accompany "Joe Turner Blues." Students will label the appropriate chords for each measure on a worksheet.

Materials: **Video Clip 4:4**
Boomwhackers, or resonator bells
12-bar blues worksheet
Chalk board

Procedures and Strategies: View Video Clip 4:4 that shows the notation of the song. Discuss the song with the students and ask what type of music it is. Explain that it is known as the Blues and originated with slaves in southern United States. The blues uses "blue notes," which are lowered (flatted), that result in a mournful or melancholy feeling. Ask students to find the blue note in the song (E flat).

Review that the primary chords in any key (I, IV, and V) are the most often used chords to add harmony to western music. Since "Joe Turner Blues" is in the key of C, the chords will be the C chord (I), the F chord (IV), and the G chord (V). Notate a C major scale on the board, and ask students to complete the I, IV, and V chords. Also discuss the difference between a V chord and a V7 chord. Review as needed.

The blues often follow a particular formula resulting in the "12-bar blues Form." Twelve bars means that there are twelve measures in each verse. The chord formula for 12 bar blues is as follows:

I chord	IV chord	I chord	V7 chord	I chord
Measures 1– 4	Measures 5-6	Measures 7-8	Measures 9-10	Measures 11-12

The text of each verse (called a chorus in the blues) has three phrases and the lyrics usually follow an "a a b" scheme where the text of the first phrase is repeated and then a different text used for the third phrase. It is also common for the text to occupy only 2-3 measures of each 4-measure phrase. The guitar or other accompanying instruments "fill" in the remainder of the phrase.

Ask the class to look at the notation of "Joe Turner Blues" on the video clip and figure out where the I, IV, and V chords are used. (The song follows the typical 12-bar blues pattern. Explain that seventh chords are often used in the blues, so the notation has a C7 and an F7 as well as the expected G7 on the V chord). Ask students to sing along as the video clip is played again.

Randomly distribute resonator bells or boomwhackers. Ask all of the students who have a note of the C chord (I) to come and stand in a group. (Check to see that all have a C, E, or G). Do the same for the F chord (IV) and the G7 chord (V7). Ask each group to play their notes to the steady beat as you conduct them, following the 12-bar blues pattern (I chord for 4 measures, IV chord for 2 measures, I chord for 2 measures, V7 chord for two measures, and I chord for the final two measures). Rehearse as needed and then add the chord accompaniment as the video is played.

Singing by Rote 5

Singing has been a mainstay of the elementary music curriculum since its beginnings in the Boston schools in the 1830s. In fact, for many years, singing was *the* major activity for elementary music. Elementary music programs were often reinstated or cut based on the children's singing performance. Although present day elementary curriculums are multifaceted, singing should and does remain a priority in quality music programs.

Almost all songs in Kindergarten and first grade are taught by *rote.* Rote teaching relies on students learning by imitating what the teacher sings. Because most children at this level do not read, and so as not to distract them, children are not given a copy of the words or music. Rote teaching of songs continues throughout the elementary grades, although it is common in upper grades to blend rote teaching with note teaching in which the students do have the music.

There are two main approaches to rote singing: the *whole song method* and the *part song method*. In the whole song method, the teacher sings the song several times, each time suggesting that the students listen for something specific (text, mood, melodic contour, tempo, etc.). The teacher then asks the students to join in singing the song when they are ready. If the song is long, the children may not learn the song adequately in a single music period, but the song can be repeated the next time the children have music class.

The part song method, as its name implies, is taught in sections, usually one phrase at a time. The part song, or phrase method, is outlined below:

1. The teacher sings the entire song to the class after getting the starting pitch.
2. If there are words the students may not understand, they should be explained.

3. The teacher sings the song again.
4. The teacher sings the first phrase and motions to class to repeat.*
5. The teacher sings the second phrase, and motions to class to repeat.
6. The teacher sings the first two phrases together and motions to class to repeat.˙
7. Steps 4 through 6 are repeated for the remainder of the song.
8. After teaching all of the phrases, the teacher sings the entire song with the class after giving a ready signal.⁺
9. The class sings the song alone after a ready signal is given.

---

* It is helpful for the teacher to show the beat (hand on chest) while singing and then gesture to the class so that they come in on the beat immediately following the ending of the phrase.
˙ Some teachers prefer to sing each phrase of the song first and then put two phrases together. Whichever technique is used, this step is beneficial for students because it enables them to "chunk" a larger portion of the song to memory.
⁺ A typical ready signal might be "One, two, ready, sing." However, the ready signal varies depending on the meter of the song and whether or not there is a pickup. In general, "ready, sing" should be given on the two beats before the singing starts.

The following guidelines should help you as you prepare to teach a rote song to the class.

Peer Teaching a Rote Song

Young children learn songs by rote, or imitation, without the music in their hands. Even after children begin to read, many songs are taught by rote. Music specialists and classroom teachers need to develop skill in teaching by rote. The following guidelines will help you prepare for your peer teaching of a rote song.

Limit your self to 5 minutes for the presentation (keep things moving).

Memorize your presentation, but you may have a copy of the song and a list of procedures to remind you of steps.

Your song must be approved ahead of time in order to avoid songs that everyone knows and to assure that everyone teaches a different song.

The sequence of the presentation is as follows:

1. Play the song through on piano (without singing. This helps you remember the tune).
2. Motivate the song by discussing its subject, origin, etc.
3. Give the starting pitches (ask class to sing "loo" with you).
4. Teacher sings the entire song alone.
5. Sing phrase one, motion to class to repeat.
6. Sing phrase two, motion to class to repeat.
7. Sing phrases one and two, motion to class to repeat.
8. Sing phrase three, motion to class to repeat.
9. Sing phrase four, motion to class to repeat.

10. Sing phrases three and four, motion to repeat.
11. Ask class to sing whole song with you after giving a ready signal.
12. Ask class to sing alone, after giving the ready signal.

Remember that if the class has difficulty at any step, you should repeat that portion before continuing. Praise the students if they do well. Practice teaching your song to friends before teaching it in class—practice does help!

Your presentation will be assessed by a rubric such as the following:

4 – confident
3 – adequate, but could be improved
2 – unsure and hesitant
1 – needs much work

The above ratings will be applied to the following criteria:

1. Plays song accurately on piano.
2. Provides motivation for students to learn the song.
3. Begins singing the song on the correct starting pitch.
4. Demonstrates melodic accuracy.
5. Demonstrates rhythmic accuracy.
6. Provides opportunity for repeated experience with song.
7. Monitors student learning and student behavior.
8. "Get Ready" signal given properly.
9. Shows evidence of preparation.
10. Teaches with enthusiasm.

Out-of-Tune Singers

Most young children love to sing. However, three year olds may go through a "shy" stage where they do not want to sing in front of other children or adults. The teacher, caregiver, or parent can encourage young children to sing by selecting action songs, silly songs, and all types of singing games that children naturally enjoy. Some children do not learn to match pitch (sing in tune) by the time they enter Kindergarten. We refer to these students as uncertain singers or out-of-tune singers. Students should never be ridiculed because of their inability to sing, but should be encouraged and praised when they do sing correctly. Individual attention is needed to assist students in correctly matching pitch. Research indicates that children can be taught to match pitch more easily before they reach the age of eight or nine. Therefore, it is essential for teachers to know the reasons for out-of-tune singers and techniques for improving pitch matching ability of young singers.

Reasons for Out-of-Tune Singers

1. Lack of musical background resulting in inattention to pitch and failure to recognize pitch changes. Students at this stage do not realize when the pitch is going up or down.

2. Lack of maturity resulting in failure to find the singing voice and to coordinate vocal muscles with the pitches heard. These students can hear pitch changes, but do not know what to do with the vocal apparatus to match a pitch.

rare

3. A low speaking voice resulting in discomfort in matching tones at the level demanded by the teacher and the class. This is fairly rare among students.

4. Psychological inhibition toward singing caused by attitudes of peers and adults reacting to the child's unsuccessful attempts to sing. This is the most prevalent cause for out-of-tune singing.

Helps for Out-of-Tune Singers

Siren

1. Provision of regular singing experiences that arouse a child's desire to sing.
2. Imitation of familiar sounds to assist a child in finding his/her singing voice and in recognizing higher and lower sounds.
3. Frequent repetition of familiar songs and phrases of songs.
4. Singing songs including tone-matching sections such as question and answer phrases, echo games, or musical dialogue. (See "Doggie, Doggie" below)
5. Using melody instruments to discover differences in pitch and for playing simple melodies.
6. Matching a child's pitch on piano or song bells and having him/her play and sing various pitches.
7. Using hand and body motions to show pitch differences/changes.
8. Using hand puppets and visual aids to lessen psychological inhibition.

"Doggie, Doggie" is an excellent song for pitch matching. The first soloist sings with a dog puppet and the second soloist holds a rawhide bone or clave to represent the bone. The "dog" then chooses the next "dog" soloist and the person with the bone chooses another child to have the bone.

"Doggie, Doggie"

Class sings

Dog - gie, Dog - gie, Where's your bone?

Solo

Some - one stole it from my home.

Class sings

Who stole the bone?_____

2nd Solo

I stole the bone._____

Movement 6

Children love to move. It has often been said that children have boundless energy. Part of the reason for that is because children have difficulty sitting for long periods of time. Classroom teachers should be aware that children need to move, and should provide ample opportunity for movement activities during the entire school day in addition to scheduled music time. Movement promotes cooperation, aids in socialization, releases energy, deepens cultural understanding, assists in internalization of music concepts, and provides important links to creativity.

Many types of music *make* us want to move. It is difficult to listen to bluegrass without tapping your foot. Rock 'n' Roll makes us want to dance. Some music makes us want to sway or clap to the beat. You no doubt have observed a toddler watching a movie. When the music begins, she immediately begins to bounce to the music. These are all examples of the natural connection between movement and music. Music is usually considered an *aural* art because it is related to the sense of hearing. However, music is also a *kinesthetic* art because our body often reacts physically when music is present.

Classroom teachers may be reluctant to incorporate movement into the daily routine because they do not feel confident to lead movement activities or because they fear students will have an opportunity to misbehave. However, if simple ground rules are established, students and teachers alike can experience the shared joy that movement can bring. Make students aware of their *self-space*, which is also referred to as personal space. Self-space can be described as all of the space someone occupies with arms stretched out when they spin in a circle. Children should avoid running into other children or objects in the room when in their self-space. Other movement activities require shared space. Make sure that students know the space limitations for movement activities before they actually begin moving.

Leading Movement Methods

Laban movement analysis is a notation system that Rudolph Laban developed to chart movement elements. He defines movement as having weight, having a time element, and taking place in space. The weight in music corresponds to dynamic levels of loud, soft, or getting gradually louder (*crescendo*) or gradually softer (*decrescendo*). The time element is the tempo of the music, and the space element relates to pitch in music (high, medium, or low). The **Alexander Technique** and **Body Mapping** are methods that train students to move in physiologically correct ways to reduce tension caused by misuse, poor posture, or inefficient movements. The aim is to make students move in a more natural, comfortable manner.

Emile Jaques-Dalcroze has undoubtedly had more influence on the ways we incorporate movement in music classes than any other person. His approach, detailed later in this book, uses movement to aid students in internalizing music concepts, which enables them to be more expressive. Dalcroze emphasized rhythmic movement, aural and solfege training, and incorporated games and activities to get students to freely improvise movement to accompany various styles of music.

Locomotor versus Non-locomotor Movement

Children need experiences in both locomotor and non-locomotor movements. A *locomotor* movement occurs when you travel from one spot to another. Locomotor movements include walking, running, marching, hopping, tiptoeing, skipping, and galloping. Although most Kindergarten children can accomplish these movements, some may have difficulty skipping at that age. It is important to remember that children most accurately chant rhythms, and then clap rhythms, before they accurately step rhythms. Research suggests that it is also helpful for children to experience patting the beat with both hands before asking children to march to the beat. *Non-locomotor* or *axial* movements occur when the body is fixed in place (so the body forms an axis). Examples include snapping, clapping, patting (*patschen*), stamping, bending, swaying, and stepping in place.

Free versus Structured Movement

Movement can also be classified as free or structured. *Free* or *creative* movement occurs when children improvise movement according to the way the music makes them feel like moving. It is important to remember that children will be more creative if they have developed a repertoire of movements from previous activities. Teachers should set some boundaries for behavior and classroom management by leading children to discover their personal space, inform them if some areas of the room are off-limits because of safety concerns, and so forth. It is helpful to provide imagery that assists the children. For example, you might ask: "Can you move like a rabbit that is afraid?" or "Can you move like a tired pony?" Stories, poems, or pictures can also be used to stimulate creative movement.

Structured movement occurs when specific movements are prescribed, such as "move four steps forward," or "clap right hands with your partner." Generally, the older the children the more structured the movements become. However, it is important to continue to encourage free movement as well. Students in upper grades often move more readily if they have experienced a variety of movement activities in previous grades and if activities are approached as "games" rather than as "dances."

Fingerplays

Young children enjoy fingerplays because they are humorous and fun. Unlike many other movement activities, fingerplays can be performed while the children are sitting. They are beneficial in developing fine-motor control and for exercising small muscles. Children perform the motions to fingerplays as the rhyme is chanted.

"Two Little Blackbirds"
Two little blackbirds sitting on a hill
(*thumb on each hand flutters*)
One named Jack, and one named Jill.
(*raise one thumb, then the other*)
Fly away Jack. Fly away Jill
(*one hand flies behind back, then the other one*)
Come back Jack. Come back Jill.
(*one thumb comes back out, then the other one*)

Edwards, Linda; Bayless, Kathleen M.; Ramsey, Marjorie E., *Music: A Way of Life for the Young Child*, 5th Ed., © 2005. Reprinted by permission of Pearson Education, Inc., New York, New York.

Singing Games

There is a vast repertoire of singing games from countries around the world. The song lyrics often imply the actions that make up the game or activity. The following game is a favorite of American children who have played it.

"Button and the Key"

Down comes Ma - ry, down comes she.

She is hid - ing the but - ton and the key.

Who has the but - ton? I have the but - ton!

Who has the key? I have the key!

Game: Children are seated in a circle. One child is "it" and hides her/his eyes while the song is sung. A second child has a button and a third child has a key. They move behind the children and drop the key and the button in the hands of two of the children. When all sing "Who has the button," the child with the button sings alone "I have the button." When the children sing "Who has the key," the child with the key sings alone "I have the key." The child who is "it" guesses who has the button and the key. A new child becomes "it" and the children with the button and the key give them to two other children when the song is repeated.

"A Sailor Went to Sea," "Clap Your Hands," "If You're Happy," and "The Old Gray Cat" are other examples of singing games included in this book.

Choksy, Lois *Kodaly Method, The Comprehensive Music Education From Infant to Adult*, 1st Ed., © 1974. Reprinted by permission of Pearson Education, Inc., New York, New York.

Passing Game

"Button You Must Wander"

But - ton, you must wan - der, wan - der, wan - der,

But - ton, you must wan - der ev - 'ry - where.

Bright eyes will find you, sharp eyes will find you,

But - ton you must wan - der ev - 'ry - where.

Game: A child who is "it" sits in the center of the circle and closes his/her eyes while a button is given to a child. As the song is sung, all the children pretend to pass the button as the child with the button does pass it on. At the end of the song "it" guesses who has the button. The person with the button becomes "it" when the song is repeated.

Choksy, L.; Brummitt, D., *120 Singing Games & Dances for Elementary Schools,* 1st Ed., © 1987.
Reprinted by permission of Pearson Education, Inc., New York, New York.

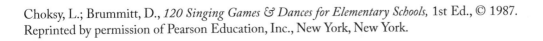

Hand Jive

A hand jive involves hand movements and claps and can sometimes result in fairly complicated ostinato patterns. After you learn "Four White Horses" you can accompany the song with the detailed six-beat hand jive pattern performed in groups of four students.

"Four White Horses"

Four white hors - es on the riv - er, Hey, hey,— hey,

'ope to-mor-row, 'Ope to-mor-row is a rain-y day.

Come on up— to the shal-low bay. Shal-low bay— is a

ripe ba-na-na, 'Ope to-mor-row is a rain-y day.

Movement: Children stand in groups of four with two sets of facing partners. One group is couple 1, the other couple 2. The following six beat pattern continues throughout the song:

1. clap own hands

2. clap partner's hands (couple 1 above, couple 2 below)

3. clap own hands

4. clap side partner's hands (shoulder height, palms out)

5. clap own hands

6. clap partner's hands (couple 1 below, couple 2 above)

"My Landlord" is another example of a hand jive song included in this book.

Choksy, Lois, *The Kodaly Content*, 1st Ed., © 1981. Reprinted by permission of Pearson Education, Inc., New York, New York.

Circle Games and Dances

"Here Comes a Bluebird"

Here comes a blue-bird in through my win-dow,

Hey, dee-dle dum-a-day, day, day.

Take a lit-tle part-ner, hop in the gar-den,

Hey, dee-dle dum-a-day, day, day.

Game: Children stand in a circle with hands joined and raised to form the windows. One child, the "bluebird," walks in and out of the windows for the first two phrases. On the phrase "Take a little partner" the bluebird takes the hand of the nearest person and they hop together in a small circle until the song ends. When the song is repeated both partners go in and out the windows separately and each choose a partner and hop in the circle. Continue until all are chosen.

"Teddy Bear," "Bow Wow Wow," and "Great Big House" are other examples of circle games and dances included in this book.

Movement ideas with recorded music

"Havah Nagila"

Carlton, Elizabeth B, and Phyllis S Weikart, *Rhythmically Moving 4*. Ypsilanti, MI: High/Scope Press, 1997. (Also accessible on youtube at https://www.youtube.com/watch?v=Vx9DTDDG8lc.

Dance Steps: The six-beat Hora:

Students stand in a circle with hands on hips (or join hands).

1. Step to the left
2. Right foot behind the left
3. Step to the left.
4. Hop on left foot while kicking right leg in front of left.
5. Step to the right
6. Hop on right foot while kicking left leg in front of right

Repeat throughout the song.

The two lesson ideas that follow are examples that incorporate movement to recorded music. Teachers can create similar lessons adapted to students' age ranges and ability levels.[1]

---

[1] The two lessons were adapted by Dr. Alan Gumm, Professor of Music Education, Central Michigan University, Mt. Pleasant, MI.

How Would You Move
Adapted from sequences by Gar Richter and David Wood

Grade Level: all levels and ages
Music Concepts: beat, tempo. rhythm, cadence
Movement Concepts: shared space, direction (in/out, up/down), shape, force/weight, flow
Objectives: *perform* and *create* through movement
National Standards: #6 Listen, analyze, and describe; #8 Relate to other arts/disciplines (dance)
Materials: drum, cymbal, or bass metallophone; recording of slow music such as Stravinsky's *Firebird Suite* "Berceuse" or Schumann's *Adagio for Strings*; floor space; poetry

Procedure – Strategy

1. Ask students to follow a drum beat and show how they would move if . . .

   a. they were tired;
   b. they had drunk too much soda pop;
   c. one leg was hurt;
   d. the floor was hot;
   e. the floor was sticky;
   f. the wind was blowing hard, etc.

   . . . and to stop moving when they hear a rhythmic signal that interrupts the steady beat. Monitor and reinforce that students maintain equidistant *movements* that *balance* the room, and that their movements reflect the "move if" statement in direction, shape, force, and flow.

2. Ask students to be ready to describe the direction, shape, force, and flow of movement as they move to a drum beat in shared space or in a circle to different mood or emotion words spoken by the teacher such as:

   Peace, Anger, Depression, Joy, Delight, Sadness, Embarrassment, Optimism, Rejoicing.

   Monitor and reinforce appropriate movements and descriptions (for example, positive moods/emotions are outward and up, negative moods/emotions are inward and down).

3. Ask students to identify movements in a poem read by the teacher and then to reflect the movements in self or shared space. Play the recorded slow music in the background to set a calm mood. Stop and start the music when you want the students to move or stop in place. For example, read *Fog* by Carl Sandburg with a few students in self-space to represent the city buildings and the others in shared-space to represent the fog:

   The fog comes
   on little cat feet.

   It sits looking
   over harbor and city
   on silent haunches
   and then moves on.

Reprinted by permission of Alan Gumm.

Music Box Dancer

Grade Level: upper elementary
Music Concepts: melody, form, timbre
National Standards: #6. Listen/analyze/describe music. #8. Relate to other arts/disciplines (movement, dance, behavior management)
Materials: a recording of "Music Box Dancer" by Frank Mills; a drum; floor space for movement
Previous Knowledge/Experiences: How Would You Move" lesson or other experience with self-space and shared-space movement concepts

Procedure—Strategy

1. Have students find self-space in the room and move isolated "hinges" or joints of the body individually and in different combinations within the time span of different tempos or counts (within a count of 2 = fast, 5 = medium, 10 = slow).

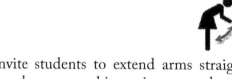

2. Invite students to extend arms straight out to the side. To the beat of the drum move hinges in an up-down motion starting with the farthest knuckle on one side through each hinge one at a time to the end knuckles on the other side-repeat with increasing tempo of the drum. The goal is for the coordinated motions to become a steady wave of motion. Reinforce the best examples until every student shows coordination of specific hinge movements into an overall wave motion.

3. Have students explore other isolated hinge dance moves, such as "the robot," mild break dancing, or Michael Jackson's "moon walk." Monitor and reinforce until all improve in coordination, agility, and body spatial awareness.

4. Have students choose a unique set of hinge movements and adapt them to the form of *Music Box Dancer*. They freeze on the repetitive piano introduction and interludes, use self-space axial hinge movements when the melody occurs alone, and use locomotor shared-space hinge movements when drums and vocals are added. (You may wish to add walking to the beat to the hinge movements they choose). When students have selected their desired movements, start the recording. Nonverbally influence improved movement by scrutinizing each student's movements and pointing out best examples until everybody moves creatively and appropriately to the form of the music.

Reprinted by permission of Alan Gumm.

5. Have students reflect on the order of movements and musical events to describe the form of the piece:

intro (freeze)
melody (self-space)
melody + *instruments* (shared space)
interlude (freeze)
melody (self-space)
melody + *instruments* (shared space)
interlude (freeze)
melody (self-space)
melody + *instruments* (shared space).

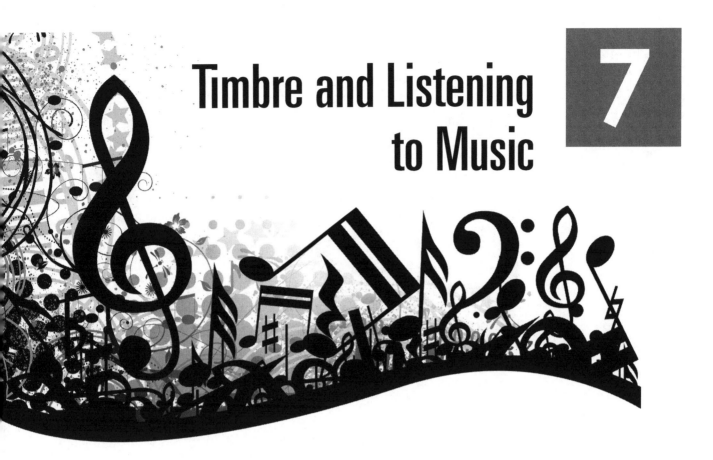

Timbre and Listening to Music

7

The distinctive sound of a particular voice or instrument is known as **timbre** or tone color. Some of the first experiences in timbre discrimination with children involve sound exploration. That is followed by recognition of 1) vocal timbre as being produced by a child, a woman, or a man; and 2) recognition of the timbre of individual instruments and families of instruments.

Sound Exploration

Students will become better listeners if they have a variety of sound exploration experiences in preschool and the early grades. Sound exploration can include traditional instruments, but often begins with *found sounds*, sounds that can be produced in the environment. Young children need lots of opportunities for sound exploration, with adult guidance rather than specific directions. Maria Montessori mastered this technique and used it for sound exploration as well as for the entire preschool curriculum. Sample sound exploration activities include:

- Taking a sound walk. This can work with preschoolers through elementary grades. Listen/discuss sounds around you as you walk through leaves, hear birds sing, observe children playing, encounter street noise, etc.
- Kitchen Orchestra. Provide pots and pans, lids, utensils and have children explore sounds. Younger children gravitate toward louder sounds, possibly because it makes them feel in control of their environment. After initial exploratory sessions, ask questions such as: "Who can find the highest sound? . . . the lowest? . . . the softest? . . . the loudest? . . . the longest? . . . the shortest?" (Use comparatives so children begin thinking conceptually).

- Animal sound compositions. Ask students to suggest animal sounds and combine them into a "composition" incorporating long and short sounds, high and low sounds, etc. With children's help, create graphic notation to represent the different sounds. Perform the composition while recording it. Let children hear the recording and suggest improvements. Perform the composition backwards, rearrange portions, etc., just as a composer would if writing a piece of music.

- Adding sound effects to poems and stories. Many children's books and poems can be used with sound exploration activities. Read the story or poem aloud and ask children to suggest sound effects to accompany the literature. This works particularly well with *haiku*, Japanese nature poems having three lines in a 5-syllable, 7-syllable, and 5-syllable format. Students can also write their own Haiku-type poem and add sound effects. Added sound effects can be limited to found sounds, vocal sounds, instrument sounds, or a combination of all three.

(See Poems for Sound Exploration on page 141)

- "Notated" sound compositions. For upper grade students, provide parameters for creating their own sound compositions and notating them in some way. An example might be to create a sound composition using at least four different sounds, at least one of which is a found sound, in an A B A form, lasting at least 20 seconds. Graphic notation may be ideal at first. Gradually work toward more standard notation, as students are able.

Timbre Recognition

Sound exploration activities, such as those listed above can help students become aware of timbre changes. Many singing games, such as "Do You Know the Muffin Man?," feature a child who hides his or her eyes and guesses the singer based on the individual timbre of the voice. Young children should be given opportunities to hear the difference between men's, women's, and children's voices. Beginning in fourth grade, the terms Soprano, Alto, Tenor, and Bass can be introduced and the various timbre types identified.

As listening skills develop, students should learn to recognize the timbre or tone color of families of instruments and individual instruments within families. Research shows that even young students can learn to recognize the timbre of individual instruments if given adequate exposure to that instrument. The basal series normally feature units on timbre recognition by family in the third grade book. Beginning instrument experiences should feature the timbre of classroom instruments. Rhythm instruments and melody instruments such as guitar, autoharp, piano, recorder, and song bells should be explored. Listening lessons, such as call charts, can be focused on individual instruments or families of instruments as well as other concepts. Traditional families of instruments include Strings, Brasses, Woodwinds, and Percussion. However, many sources now recognize Keyboards as being a separate family of instruments. Instruments from world cultures should also be included in the general music curriculum. The basal series feature many recorded examples of instruments from other cultures that can be used for timbre identification.

Listening to Music

Music seems to surround us. Whether shopping, eating at a restaurant, or watching television, we are almost continually exposed to some type of music. We can be aware of music without "attending" to it. Listening, in the correct sense of the word, implies active participation in the music, taking notice of what is happening in the music, and paying attention to details of the music. Perhaps because music is so prevalent in our society, we often treat it as background noise, and pay little or no attention to what is happening in the music. Listening to music is an activity that needs to be taught in the music classroom, just as singing or playing an instrument is taught. In fact, teaching children to listen to music may be regarded as one of the most important components of general music because it is an activity that can easily continue throughout adulthood. (Reimer, 2003: 224). As mentioned in Chapter One, the sixth National Standard in Music is "Listening to, analyzing, and describing music." If we could not listen to music, it would cease to exist.

Initial experiences with listening to music can be linked to movement activities. Ask the students to take short steps when they hear short sounds, and long steps when they hear long sounds; show with body levels when the music heard is going up or down, etc. Visual aids can also be incorporated to facilitate listening. When listening for A or B sections of music, use different color-coded shapes to show when the melody has changed, etc.

Simply playing a CD in class does not indicate that listening is taking place. In order to assess what children are hearing, we use guided listening techniques. One of the most common approaches is the use of *call charts*. A call chart gets its name from the fact that the teacher calls out a number while the music is played. The call chart is numbered so that children can attend to what is happening in the music as the number is called. Diagrams are often used because visual representations capture the children's interest. For assessment purposes, a call number can have a choice provided. For example, a diagram of a flute and a clarinet could be used and the student would circle which they were hearing. Call charts can focus on a single concept or they can include a mixture of appropriate concepts. It is essential to design age-appropriate charts so as not to discourage the listener. The latest basal series books have excellent examples of call charts. Teachers often create their own call charts to correspond to particular conceptual units. Students of all ages also enjoy creating call charts in small groups and sharing their charts with the class. See sample call charts for "The Old Gumpie Cat" from *Cats*, "Scene" from *Swan Lake*, and "You and Me" by David Matthews Band on the following pages.

Another guided listening technique is the use of *listening maps*. These are similar to call charts in that prominent features of the music are displayed on the map, but numbers are not called. Students follow the map as the music is played. Informal assessment can occur by discussing the music following the listening exercise. As with call charts, teachers and students can create their own listening maps using diagrams, icons, words, or other symbols.

It is important for teachers to remember that if they talk while music is playing, the students are unable to listen to the music. Listening lessons should be planned so that all necessary talking takes place before or after listening to the music. A common mistake that teachers make is to plan listening lessons that are too long to hold the attention of the students. Young children will need practice in actively listening for more than a minute or so. Begin with short excerpts and gradually increase the length as students show they are able to concentrate longer.

Listening Lesson Assignment

1. Choose a piece of music that you would like to share with students. Consider all kinds and styles of music—pop, jazz, classical, music of other cultures, musicals, children's music, etc.
2. Listen to the music several times and pick out prominent music concepts. The best way to do this is to listen for changes in the music. For instance—are there portions that are faster or slower, higher or lower, softer or louder? Is there a steady beat? Does the timbre change from one instrument to another, or from male to female singers, etc.? Does the music move in 2's (duple) or 3's (triple)? Do melodies repeat or are there contrasting sections?
3. Design a "call chart" to help children find their way through the music. Consider using pictures, diagrams, and icons so that children's attention is captured.
4. Your chart should:
   a) be interesting
   b) be short (3 or 4 minutes of a continuous excerpt)
   c) focus attention on important features of the music.
5. Include your name, title of the music, and composer or group on the chart Make a photocopy for each member of the class.
6. On a separate sheet, provide a teaching guide that includes the grade level(s) for which it is intended, concepts chosen, and the correct answers to your choices.
7. Your chart needs to have at least 8 call numbers. At least four of the eight need to provide a choice (i.e. is a saxophone or a guitar playing, etc.).
8. Practice calling the numbers as the music is playing. Try it out on friends and make adjustments as needed.
9. For class presentation you will pass out the charts, explain diagrams as needed, call out numbers as the music is played, and discuss correct answers for the choices provided.

"The Old Gumble Cat" from <u>Cats</u>

by Andrew LLyod Webber
Geffen Records 2GHS 2031

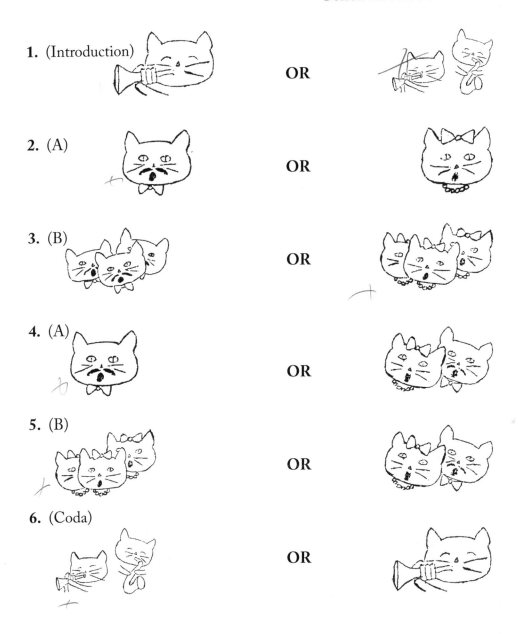

1. (Introduction)   OR

2. (A)   OR

3. (B)   OR

4. (A)   OR

5. (B)   OR

6. (Coda)   OR

"Scene" from **Swan Lake** Tchaikovsky

CALL NUMBER	WHAT DID YOU HEAR?
1. Melody played by the oboe.	1. How many phrases were in this melody? **1 2 3**
2. Another melody played by the oboe.	2. How may phrases were in this melody? **1 2 3**
3. A melody played by the horns.	3. Which shows the melodic contour?
4. A melody played by the violins and violas.	4. Which shows the melodic contour?
5. Transition section played by strings, woodwinds, and brasses.	5. Which shows the contour at the end or the transition?
6. A melody played by different instruments.	6. **a)** Last instrument to play the melody? **Flutes, Horns, or Strings** **b)** Is the whole melody played? **Yes No** **c)** The melody **crescendos, decrescendos,** or **stays to same** dynamic level?

"YOU AND ME" by Dave Matthews Band
Call Chart

Time Elapsed	Timbre	Dynamics
0:00 – 0:11 1.	 Guitar alone	soft = *p*
0:12 – 0:59 2.	 Guitar and singing	medium soft = *mp*
1:00 – 1:23 3.	+ + +	loud = *f*
1:24 – 2:04 4.	+	medium loud = *mf*
2:05 – 2:37 5.	**OR** + + + One Instrument Many Instruments	loud = *f*

2:38 – 2:59		
6.	One Singer **OR** Two Singers +	medium loud = *mf*
3:00 – 3:53		
7.	+ + + + Many Instruments	loud = f
3:54 - end		
8.		soft = *p*

Images © Shutterstock, Inc.

Listening Suggestions for Timbre. (YouTube has excellent videos of many of the following pieces).

Strings
Vivaldi, *The Four Seasons: Winter*.

Woodwinds
Jean Francoix, "Allegro Molto" from *Quartet*.
Darius Milhaud, "Jongleurs," 3rd movement from *La Cheminée du Roi René*, Op. 205.

Brasses
Handel, *Allegro for Brass Quintet*.

Percussion
John Cage, *Third Construction for Percussion Ensemble*.
Chávez, *Toccata for Percussion*, movement 3.

Keyboards
Piano: Chopin, "Minute Waltz," Op. 64, No. 1.
Organ: Bach, Toccata and Fugue in D minor, BWV 565.
Harpsichord: Rameau, "Les Tourbillons" from *Suite in D*.
Synthesizer: Jean-Jacques Perrey, *The Mexican Cactus*.

Full Orchestra (families of orchestra and individual instruments featured)
Britten, *Young Persons Guide to the Orchestra*.

Featured Instruments in a story:
Prokofiev, *Peter and the Wolf*.
Saint-Saens, *Carnival of the Animals*.

Men's and Women's Voices Alternating
Andrew Lloyd Webber, "The Old Gumbie Cat" from *Cats*.

[new] Children's Voices
Johann Strauss, *Tritsch Tratsch Polka*, sung by the Vienna Boys' Choir - YouTube

POEMS FOR SOUND EXPLORATION

A Quiet Time

Up in my room
I can sense more than hear
The tip-tip-toeing
Of shy falling rain.

Molly the Mama-cat
Two feet of stretched fur
Saws syncopated logs
With comic refrain.

The clock holds its rhythm
But doesn't intrude.
It tells me that this time
Is mine—all mine.

A few broken chords
On my brand new guitar
While the world outside
Is benign.

There Was An Old Witch

There was an old witch
Believe it if you can.
She tapped on the windows
And she ran, ran, ran.

She ran helter skelter
With her toes in the air,
Corn stalks flying from the old witch's hair.

"Swish," goes the broomstick,
"Meow," goes the cat.
"Flop," goes the hoptoad sitting on her hat.
"Whoa," chuckled I, "What fun, what fun"
Halloween night when the witches run.

New Year's Eve
FIVE . . . FOUR . . . THREE . . TWO . . .
ONE . . . MIDNIGHT!

It's gone forever that happy old year,
With Chrtistmas, Thanksgiving, and Fourth
of July.

Sound horns, ring bells, cheer and strike
gongs.
When I look back, will I laugh or cry?

Clash metal on metal, make a festival noise.
Will new days creep slowly or lift off and fly?

Let's welcome this moment, this Happy New
Year,
With Christmas, Thanksgiving, and Fourth of
July

Tumbling Jack

Tumbling jack goes clickety-clack.
Down the ladder and then comes back.
Clickety-clackety, rattle and hop.
Over and down again, flippety-flop

Song of Summer

A thrush in a bush: "Lira-lira-ling!"
A cricket in a thicket: "Zing-zing-zing!"
A frog in a bog: "Boom-boom-boom!"

A bee in a blossom: "Zoom-zoom-zoom!"
Listen, Listen! There's music all about.
Does anybody want to sing or whistle—or shout?

"Tumbling Jack," as appeared in *Music In the Education of Children* by Bessie R. Swanson.

"I Rode on a Jet," from *Exploring Music*, copyright © 1975 by Holt, Rinehart, and Winston. Reprinted with permission of Holt, Rinehart, and Winston.

"Song of Summer" as appeared in *Winds A'Blowing* by May Justus.

"A Quiet Time," by Susan Lucas as appeared in *Music In the Education of Children* by Bessie R. Swanson.

"New Year's Eve," by Matthew Alden as appeared in *Music In the Education of Children* by Bessie R. Swanson.

"There Was an Old Witch," from *This Is Music*, Book II by William R. Sur, Mary R. Tolbert, William R/ Fisher and Adeline McCall, Allyn & Bacon, 1961.

Form

8

The element of music that refers to its design or structure is ***Form***. Just as a house is made up of different rooms, a piece of music is made up of different sections. The best music examples have a balance of repetition and contrast. If music is too repetitive our brain soon ignores it. If music has no contrast, the brain also disregards it after a period of time. Skillful composers blend repetition and contrast so that a piece of music has unity.

The smallest unit of form is a ***motive***. A motive, sometimes called a musical idea, generally is made up of five to ten notes. In order for the pattern to be considered a motive, it must be used several times in the piece of music. Beethoven's *Symphony No. 5* contains the most famous example of a motive That motive, shown below, was used to unify much of the symphony and was used to symbolize victory during World War II.

Songs can also be based on a motive. Think of the tune "Polly Waddle Doodle All Day." The first five notes on, "Oh, I went down South" are immediately repeated on "for to see my Sal." The motive, one step lower, is heard again in the second phrase on "My, Sal she is." Introductions (heard before the main theme begins), interludes (between sections or verses), and codas (endings) are often based on a single motive.

The next larger unit of form is a ***phrase***, or musical thought. A phrase of a song is often four measures in length, but can be shorter or longer. There is usually a chord change, or cadence, at the end of a phrase. A phrase is indicated with a lower case letter. The first phrase is always "a." The next phrase is labeled "a" if it is exactly the same or nearly so, "b" if it is mostly different, or a^1 if it is similar. The melody is the main determining factor for determining phrase form. Analyze the phrase form of "The Elephant Song" notated below.

The correct phrase form would be a b a b because the first and third phrases are the same and the second and fourth phrases use the same notes, with a slight difference in the rhythm.

A ***Section*** or ***Period*** consists of at least two phrases and usually sounds as though the piece could conclude when the section ends. Sections of music are indicated by an upper case letter, A, B, etc. There are several main categories of sectional form. A piece that has an A section and a B section only is called ***Binary*** or ***2 part song form***. When introducing binary form to children, it is helpful to use color-coded shapes. For example, a red circle might represent A and a blue square used to represent B. Just as in phrase form, the melody determines the letter names assigned to each section.

Ternary or ***3 part song form*** is used to describe a piece of music that has an A B A sectional form. In addition to contrasting shapes, examples of Oreo cookies (cookie, filling, cookie) or a sandwich (bread, peanut butter, bread) can be used to illustrate ABA form. Children can also be asked to find "A B A" patterns in the classroom such as speaker, screen, speaker, or door, window, door.

Music that has a different melody for each section is referred to as ***Through Composed*** because the composer has used a different melody or theme for each section. The shortest through composed example would be A B C.

Yet another section form consists of repeated sections with alternating, contrasting sections between. Called a ***Rondo***, this type of form always has at least five sections which are A, B, A, C, A. Following those five sections a B section or C section or D section could occur, but a rondo always ends with an A section. During the Classical period, a "grand rondo" was frequently used. The grand rondo form is ABACABA. A rondo can be illustrated for students using different sport's players such as a basketball player to represent A, a tennis player for B, a soccer player for C, etc.

When a theme is repeated several times, but varied in some way each time it occurs, we refer to the form as ***Theme and Variations.*** The rhythm or melody, or both the rhythm and melody, can be altered for a variation. The form can be diagrammed as $AA^1A^2A^3A^4$, etc. with another A used each time the theme is repeated.

A common technique that composers use to extend a piece of music is called ***Sequence.*** A sequence in music occurs when the same melodic pattern is repeated at a different pitch level. The pitch can be lowered or raised. A sequence occurs in *America* as notated below. Notice that the melodic pattern of "Land of the Pilgrims' pride" is lowered one step from "Land where my fathers died" which immediately precedes it.

"America"

ARR . HENRY CAREY

Many other more complicated forms are used in music, but they follow the same basic principles as outlined above. Form can be determined by formally analyzing music and by listening to music. Children can easily learn to distinguish basic types of form if given sufficient practice and guidance.

Listening Suggestions for Form:
AB
Folk song, "Yankee Doodle."

ABA
Bizet, "Carillon" from *L'Arlésienne Suite No. 1*.
Copland, "Circus Music," from *Red Pony Suite*.

ABA with Introduction, Interlude, and Coda
Jean-Jacques Perrey, *The Mexican Cactus*.

ABC
Israeli folk song, "Havah Nagila."

Rondo
Kodály, "Viennese Musical Clock" from *Háry János Suite*.
Rameau, "Gigue en Rondeau" from *Suite in E minor*.

Theme and Variations
Handel," "Air with Variations," 4th movement from *Suite No. 5 in E Major*, HWV 430 – also known as "The Harmonious Blacksmith."
Mozart, "Ah, vous dirai-je Maman" KV 265 for Piano ("Twinkle, Twinkle, Little Star").

Methodologies and Lesson Planning

9

The elementary music methodologies that have gained the most attention in the United States since the 1960s are the Dalcroze method, the Orff approach, and the Kodály method. Each of these approaches is based on the work of a European musician. Although the approaches have many similarities, the differences in the approaches are striking.

Dalcroze

Émile Jaques-Dalcroze was born in Vienna in 1865 and died in 1950. His mother was a music teacher and made certain that Dalcroze was exposed to Vienna's rich cultural life. Dalcroze developed a passion for all of the arts, not just for music. His artistic endeavors included singing, composing, playing the piano, acting, writing plays, writing poetry, and conducting. At the age of 28, he became a professor at the Conservatory of Music in Geneva, Switzerland. He was concerned that his students had not developed better music sensitivity: they had limited improvisational skills, lacked ability to "hear" the music they wrote in theory classes, and evidenced little understanding of rhythmic structure and nuance. He experimented with the connections between music, movement, cognition, and physical skills, which led to his teaching of "eurhythmics." (Caldwell, 1994).

Movement became an integral part of teaching every music concept in the Dalcroze approach. This provided a kinesthetic connection between the mind and the body. Every Dalcroze lesson includes three components:

1. **Solfege**, based on a fixed *do* system in which *do* is always C.
2. **Improvisation**:
    a) Students improvise rhythms, melodies, and movements to aid in studying music and music concepts.
    b) Teachers are expected to have excellent improvisational skills at the piano or other instruments.
3. **Eurhythmics**, the rhythmic and harmonic processes used to teach Solfege and improvisation is emphasized.

It is difficult to gain a proper appreciation for Dalcroze techniques by simply reading about his method because lessons are largely based on student needs and feedback as the lesson progresses. Students show the teacher what they hear and understand through their movements and words, and the teacher responds by creating games that heighten sensitivity and awareness. These are difficult to detail in a typical lesson plan.

Dalcroze greatly influenced scholars and thinkers in fields such as preschool and elementary education, modern dance, theater, and opera. Montessori borrowed many of Dalcroze's ideas for her preschool curriculum, Kodály was influenced by his use of solfege, and Orff capitalized on improvisational aspects of the Dalcroze ideology.

Sample activities using the Dalcroze approach include:

1. Students will create a hand gesture to accompany saying their first name. Select several students to say their name and have the class imitate the gesture and voice inflections. Repeat until students have mastered the nuances of the vocal timbre and the gesture.
2. Select a student to walk from one side of the room to the other in any manner he chooses. The teacher accompanies the movement with a hand drum. Solicit responses about how the student walked (steadily, haltingly, rapidly, slowly, heavily, and so forth). Select other students to walk "differently." Discuss each and the differences observed. Notice that the teacher doesn't tell students how to walk, but the teacher can guide the discussion concerning the differences.
3. Students improvise movements to accompany the teacher's piano improvisations. Several styles and different tempi are played. Discuss factors that influenced students' choice of movements.

Kodály

Zoltán Kodály was born in Hungary in 1882 and died in 1967. In 1905, Kodály and his good friend, composer Béla Bartók, traveled throughout Hungary collecting folk songs. Kodály was also a composer and arranged many of the folk songs that he discovered and quoted them in his other compositions.

When Kodály began working with music educators, in the 1930s, he based his method on general principles as outlined below. He contributed the basic ideas of the method, but individual teachers refined Kodály's ideas into a workable, teachable method. It is important to note that Kodály borrowed most of his ideas from others. Although often referred to as Kodály hand signs, the hand signs were actually developed in England, the rhythm syllables he used were of French origin, etc. Kodály's fame resulted because he combined many proven techniques into a cohesive, structured method.

1. The Kodály approach emphasizes music education **early** in the child's life (nursery school) and begins with songs and games.
2. **Music literacy** is the primary goal of the Kodály approach. Literacy is taught though rhythmic exercises, solfege training, listening to music, and development of "inner hearing," the ability to "hear" sounds from notation or from hand signs even though the physical sound is not present.
3. The approach is very **sequential**—teaching is arranged so that new concepts are based on previous musical learning.
4. The **folk music** of a country (folk songs, games, and dances) is the main material used in the Kodály approach.
5. **Singing** is the main activity for learning music concepts and is featured in every lesson.
6. Tools of the Kodály approach are **Curwen hand signals**, **solfege syllables** using moveable "*do*," and **duration syllables** (ta, ti ti, etc.).
7. The descending minor third—so to mi—is the first interval learned, followed by la.
8. <u>Pentatonic</u> tonality is the starting point. Major and minor scales are learned later.
9. The Kodály approach to music education has been adapted for use in countries around the world.

Most of the activities in Chapter 2 and 3 of this book are based on a Kodály-inspired sequence of concepts. The strength of the Kodály method is that students become excellent musicians who can sing well, sight read fluently, and think musically.

(See Lessons 2:14 "Rover" and 3:10 "Rain, Rain" for examples of lessons emphasizing the Kodály approach).

Orff

Carl Orff was born in Germany in 1895 and died in 1982. Although a composer, Orff had a love for dance, and envisioned movement and music as being intertwined. The Orff approach sprung from his work in the theater, which combined music and dance. The following characteristics summarize Orff's ideas.

1. Orff called his approach to music education an "elemental" one—meaning that it starts with the most simple, natural aspects of the music, such as the pulse, or basic beat.
2. The Orff approach uses speech sounds, chants, and body movements.
3. Sequential music learnings are not a feature of the Orff approach as he designed it (although teachers often add sequential skills).
4. Body movements include snapping, clapping, patschen (slapping thighs), and stamping. Children also improvise movement dances to accompany songs.
5. Echoing, body movements, vocal, rhythmic, and instrumental ostinati, canons, and borduns (open 5ths) are all important means of music making.

6. The main goal of the Orff approach is on creative improvisation. This is accomplished through playing of the xylophones, metallophones, and glockenspiel (melody instruments), as well as with drums, tambourines, blocks, etc. (non-tuned percussion instruments).

7. Bars on all of the melody instruments are removable so beginning experiences with the instruments use only needed bars.

8. Pentatonic tonality is the starting point in the Orff approach. By removing the fourth and seventh tones (bars) of the major scale, a pentatonic scale is formed which enables children to improvise with no harsh dissonances.

9. Although children sing as they play, singing is not the principal objective in the Orff approach.

10. Music literacy is not a major goal. However, Orff wanted students to be able to write down their improvisations so they could remember them.

11. "Orffestrations" are part of the approach. These are songs that have instrumental parts and body movements added to them in a written score.

12. Orff is useful with younger children for illustrating stories and poetry with sound effects and for creating mood.

(See Lessons 2:17 "Rain Is Falling Down" and 2:20 "Speech Canon" for examples of lessons emphasizing the Orff approach).

A typical Orff activity would be to begin by teaching a folk song to students. Then, through the use of improvisation (movement, as well as rhythmic, and melodic), add layers of sound with varying ostinato patterns. Children who are not playing an instrumental part might then improvise a movement sequence to accompany the song. The teacher might add an improvisation on the recorder and teach that to selected students. The end result is a multi-layered piece that can be performed, altered further, etc. Elementary students enjoy playing the instruments and the Orff approach provides a perfect opportunity to nourish student creativity.

Specific Method or Eclecticism

In reality, there are very few teachers who use only one of the methodologies. There are many teachers who prefer one method over another, but the lines separating the methodologies have become more blurred in recent years. For example, most Orff teachers include some solfege work and many use duration syllables. Many Kodály teachers incorporate Orff instruments and emphasize improvisation. It is hard to imagine an elementary music teacher who does not include movement strategies, a la Dalcroze, to reinforce conceptual learning. Although some experts argue that the various methods are too different to be combined in meaningful ways, the eclectic approach, choosing the best techniques from each approach, seems to work for many teachers.

Lesson Planning

Successful teachers make lesson planning a priority. Long-range planning is necessary to establish goals for what you want students to be able to do in a month, a semester, or a year. Daily lesson planning should be based on specific objectives to enable you to reach the long-term goals. Lesson plans should be designed to motivate the learners, should feature a variety of music activities, provide positive, musical experiences for the students, and should have obvious connections to the National Standards for music education. Individual teachers may use different lesson plan formats, but all should specify what the students are expected to learn in the lesson.

A fairly standard lesson plan will have the following components:

1. **Concept statement** that identifies the conceptual focus for the lesson.
2. **Behavioral objective** that specifies learner outcomes. (See examples below).
3. **Materials** that are needed to teach the lesson effectively.
4. **Procedures** that indicate what the teacher is doing, step by step.
5. **Skills and Activities** that list what the students are doing, step by step.
6. **Evaluation** or **Assessment** activity to measure if, and how well, the students have learned what you expected them to learn.

Beginning teachers seem to have more difficulty writing effective behavioral objectives than formulating the other lesson plan components. Behavior objectives have three parts. They specify learner outcomes by stating:

1. a **verb** denoting observable action
2. the **conditions** under which the action takes place
3. the desired level of **achievement**.

Action verbs that identify precisely what students are to do, such as "will clap" or "will sing" are preferred over generic terminology such as "will be able to."

The following examples use all three of the above requirements:

1. Upon hearing ten short songs in binary or ternary form, the student will correctly identify the form of eight of them.
2. After listening to the opening of the second movement of Beethoven's Symphony No. 8, the student will correctly clap the melodic rhythm.
3. After learning "Marching to Pretoria" the students will correctly march to the beat while singing the song.

Behavioral objectives are always stated in terms of what the learner does and not what the teacher does. They should indicate what the students are expected to accomplish in the lesson.

Chapter References

Caldwell, Timothy. *Expressive Singing: Dalcroze Eurhythmics for Voice*. Englewood Cliffs, NJ: Prentice Hall, 1994.

Choksy, Lois et. al. *Teaching Music in the Twenty-First Century*. Upper Saddle River, NJ: Prentice Hall, 2001.

Houlahan, Mícheál, and Philip Tacka. *Kodály Today*. NY: Oxford press, 2008.

Steen, Arvida. *Exploring Orff: A Teacher's Guide*. NY: Schott Music Publishing, 1992.

Music for Special Learners

One of the challenges of effective teaching is that every class is made up of children with differing abilities and capacities for learning. The majority of classes include children with disabilities of one type or another and legislation mandates that these children receive instruction in a regular music classroom setting when possible.

Legislative efforts to benefit special education students began in 1975 with the passage of PL 94-142, The Education for All Handicapped Children Act. This law stated that handicapped children would be provided a "free appropriate public education" in the "least restrictive environment."[1] The law stipulated that an Individualized Education Program (IEP) be established for every student needing special education. The IEP specifies instructional goals and services the school will provide the child and is determined by a committee including special education personnel, the child's teacher, administrators, and parents. Music teachers not only need to be aware of a child's IEP, but also should expect to be a part of the process to help ensure that proper placement is made and that instructional needs are met.

Although not specifically mentioned in the law, the term **"mainstreaming"** came to signify that special education students would be placed in the regular classroom for at least a portion of the school day. Initially, this often meant placing those students in music, art, and physical education classes, but few other subjects. As time passed, mainstreaming gradually assumed a wider meaning and age-appropriate placements in regular classroom settings became more standard. As special education students spent more time in the regular classroom, the term mainstreaming was replaced with **"inclusion."** Although inclusion does not have a precise definition, it is usually thought of

---

[1] See *U.S. Statutes at Large* 89 (1975): 773-96.

as placing students with a disability into age-appropriate regular classrooms and bringing special services to them in the classroom.[2] Inclusion further implies that a student spends a majority of the day in a regular educational setting.

The Americans with Disabilities Act (ADA) PL 101-336, passed in 1990, prohibited discrimination in employment practices for individuals with disabilities and guaranteed that services provided in public places, including public and private schools, must be available and accessible to individuals with disabilities. Amendments to PL 94-142 were also passed the same year. Known as IDEA, this law, PL 101-476 The Education of the Handicapped Act Amendments of 1990, changed the designation of "handicapped children" to "children with disabilities."[3] IDEA also specified that, by the time students were sixteen, the IEP must include transition services that would be provided. With the passage of IDEA, a free appropriate education was guaranteed to disabled students aged three to twenty-one. IDEA was reauthorized in 2004 and new rules passed in 2006. Present language includes that "Disability is a natural part of human experience and in no way diminishes the right of individuals to participate in or contribute to society."[4]

IDEA identifies the following disabilities as requiring special education services:

- Mental retardation
- Hearing impairments, including deafness
- Speech or language impairments
- Visual impairments, including blindness
- Emotional disturbance
- Orthopedic impairments
- Autism
- Traumatic brain injury
- Other health impairments
- Learning disabilities

Children may be classified as having one of the above disabilities or may have a combination of them. Labels seem to be a necessity, but over time can take on derogatory meanings. For this reason, labels change frequently. For instance, many states no longer use the term "mental retardation," but have replaced it with terms such as cognitive impairment. Although labels are used to identify disabilities, it is important to value every child as being a unique individual with unique abilities and disabilities. For this reason, "people first" language should be used when referring to students with special needs. Instead of saying an autistic girl or a blind boy, we should say "a girl with autism" or "a boy who is blind."

Improving Access in the Music Classroom for Students with Special Needs

For all of the reasons that we teach music to so-called normal children, we also need to teach music to students with disabilities. In addition, many special education students seem to have a special affinity for music or the other arts. Music can

[2] Bernstorf, Elaine, and Betty Welsbacher, "Helping Students in the Inclusive Classroom," *Music Educators Journal*, 82, no. 5 (March 1996): 21–2.
[3] See *U.S. Statutes at Large* 104 (1990): 1103–45.
[4] Public Law 108–446, Sec. 682(C). Accessed at www.ed.gov.

also be used in therapeutic ways, whether to calm an autistic child, or provide an outlet for a child with ADHD to expel extra energy. Characteristics of children with specific disabilities and some ways in which music can be used effectively with those students are outlined below.

Cognitive Impairments

Although cognitively impaired is a recognized category of special education in some states, many still use the terms mentally retarded or mentally impaired. The American Association on Mental Retardation (AAMR) defines mental retardation as "a disability characterized by significant limitations both in intellectual functioning and in adaptive behavior as expressed in conceptual, social, and practical adaptive skills" which has its onset before the age of 18.[5]

The classification of mentally impaired (MI) students has traditionally been based on an IQ of 70 to 75 or below. However, current practice dictates that in addition to the IQ score, students designated as cognitively or mentally impaired must have adaptive behavior limitation in two or more areas. Adaptive behaviors include the areas of conceptual skills such as ability to read, write, and use language; social skills such as taking responsibility, following rules, having self-esteem, and establishing/maintaining interpersonal relationships; and practical skills such as managing money, using the telephone, toileting, eating, and dressing.

Cognitively impaired students have the potential to develop skills and learn, but they do so at a slower pace than regular children. They may also need more repetition than normal children. Obviously, the more severe the disability, the more difficult it is for them to grasp concepts.

Cognitively impaired students often have a low frustration threshold resulting from failed attempts to achieve at the level desired by the teacher. The master teacher structures the environment so that the mentally impaired can achieve small successes that can be rewarded and built upon for future success.

Tips for Improving Access:

- *Use verbal or auditory cues to improve attention and motivation*
- *Incorporate more repetition, a slower pace, and "chunk" information to increase memory*
- *Use music to enhance self-concept, release energy, facilitate motor coordination, and promote social development skills*
- *Choose limited-range, action songs, and cumulative songs*
- *Use color-coding and icons to simplify music vocabulary and notation*

Hearing Impairments, Including Deafness

Hearing loss affects nearly 17 in 1,000 children under the age of 18. Hearing loss of the outer ear can be corrected with surgery or improved with hearing aids, but inner ear losses often produce sound distortions that cannot be corrected. IDEA classifies a hearing impairment as a hearing loss severe enough to impact the

---

[5] Accessed at http://www.aamr.org/Policies/faq_mental_retardation.shtml.

student's academic performance and ability to process language, thereby requiring special services. The greatest challenge for hearing impaired/deaf students is communicating with people who hear. Some deaf students learn to speak, but others rely on speech reading (lip reading), cued speech, and writing to communicate.

Hearing impaired and deaf students, including children who communicate with sign language, often are included in music classrooms. Hearing impaired students depend on the vibration of sound to convey the pitch, duration, intensity, and timbre of music. Although vibrations may be amplified by hearing aids, hearing impaired students respond best to loud, low sounds. Bass drums, bass xylophones, and tympani can be used for initial experiences in music. As one might expect, hearing impaired students often have trouble singing in tune and they tend to have a lower, more limited range than other singers. Expect that hearing impaired students will respond more easily to rhythmic than tonal concepts.

Tips for Improving Access:

- *Use a normal speaking tone and speak slowly*
- *Speak directly to a person who is deaf, not to the interpreter*
- *Check FM loop microphone frequently for volume and distortion control*
- *Repeat questions if child cannot see the person speaking*
- *Play melodies an octave or two lower (bass xylophone, low octaves of piano)*
- *Use hand levels to show pitch differentiations*
- *Show dynamic levels visually with a hand drum*

Speech or Language Impairments

Nearly 20% of special education students have a speech disorder or other language impairment. Speech disorders include articulation difficulties, odd voice quality, absence of intensity levels, and fluency problems. Students with language disorders may have difficulty with language use, language comprehension, or language expression. Language disorders are common among children with Down Syndrome, cerebral palsy, cognitive impairment, autism, and hearing impairments.

It is essential for music teachers to know what students have speech impairments so they can aid those students. Music and speech have many commonalities. Among these are rhythm, phrasing, dynamics, pitch levels, timbre, pacing, and accents. Students can sometimes correct speech problems if they know how these elements function in music and then transfer that knowledge to correct speech. Children with speech and language impairments can participate and be very successful in music.

Tips for Improving Access:

- *Set an example by using clear articulation*
- *Avoid interrupting children although it may take them longer to respond*
- *Record and playback voices so they can understand how they sound to others*
- *Incorporate speech games into music class focusing on articulation, fluency, and intensity levels*
- *Use singing to increase verbal output and arouse emotions to motivate speech*

Visual Impairments, Including Blindness

IDEA defines visual impairments as visual loss that, even with correction, adversely affects a child's educational performance. Students who are visually impaired or have low vision have some usable vision although they have less information to rely on than those who see well. Legally blind students are those who have less than 20/200 vision in the better eye with the best corrective lens or those who have a limited field of vision less than 20 degrees at the widest point. Visually impaired students have a normal IQ range and are socially and emotionally within the normal range. However, they often have less opportunity for social relationships and are less likely to initiate social interaction than other students.

Teachers should speak directly to a blind person in a normal tone of voice and alert them when entering or leaving a room. When guiding a blind person, let them take your arm and warn them of any obstacles in their path. Low hanging lights and signs should be removed when possible. Avoid clutter in the room and keep materials well organized and in the same locations unless you inform the blind student. Teach classmates that they should not pet or play with a working guide or service dog.

Louis Braille invented a music Braille system as well as Braille for reading printed material. For performance purposes, the Braille music has to be read ahead of time and memorized. Therefore, it is not always practical to reproduce materials such as method books in music Braille. The National Library Service for the Blind and Physically Handicapped, a division of the Library of Congress, maintains a Braille score collection and will transcribe textbooks or music scores into Braille free of charge. Although a free service, it takes time to produce materials in Braille, so teachers need to order materials at least a semester in advance. The library also offers audio recordings for courses in piano, organ, accordion, recorder, voice, beginning guitar, and music theory. The toll-free telephone number for the library is 1-800-424-8567.

Tips for Improving Access:

- *Seat students where they see best*
- *Use large, touchable visuals and large print books*
- *Allot additional time to Braille readers*
- *Warn students when changes are made in classroom seating or environment*
- *Use rote learning, echo clapping, and call and response singing when possible*
- *Orff instruments and other instruments with longer bars for lower pitches are helpful when performing*
- *Verbalize more than normal*

Emotional Disturbance or Behavioral Disorder

Most professionals prefer the term "behavioral disorder" rather than IDEA's classification of "emotional disturbance" to describe students whose behavior adversely affects the learning environment. Behavior disorders can be classified as externalizing or internalizing.[6] Externalizing behaviors are characterized by overt,

---

[6] Hunt, N. and K. Marshall, *Exceptional Children and Youth: An Introduction to Special Education,* Boston: Houghton Mifflin, 2005.

antisocial, aggressive, disruptive, noncompliant actions such as hitting, scratching, biting, having temper tantrums, throwing objects, setting fires, or harming animals. Internalizing behaviors result in withdrawing from others, fantasizing, crying, and showing feelings of depression, sadness, or fear. Students with internalizing behavior problems may frequently complain or cry, daydream, rarely speak, exhibit irregular sleeping patterns, show little facial emotion, and prefer to play alone. Students with behavioral disorders may have normal intelligence, but rarely do well in school, often have few friends, and may have difficulty getting along with parents, teachers, or other adults.

Tips for Improving Access:

- *State desired behavior in a positive way*
- *Establish classroom rules and enforce them consistently*
- *Analyze causes of disruptive behavior and alleviate them when possible*
- *Realize that different music styles may elicit different behaviors*
- *Incorporate stimulating activities such as playing drums to release pent-up energy*
- *Begin lessons with aggressive music and gradually shift to calmer styles*

Orthopedic Impairments and Other Health Impairments

Orthopedic impairments refer to physical impairments and include both neurological and musculoskeletal conditions. Neurological conditions include cerebral palsy, spina bifida, seizure disorders, and traumatic brain injuries. Musculoskeletal conditions include muscular dystrophy, juvenile rheumatoid arthritis and amputations. The impact that a physical disability has on a child's learning varies greatly and ranges from minimal impact to extreme impact on social, emotional, and academic skills.

- *Let students do whatever they can for themselves, but teacher and other students assist when needed*
- *Avoid leaning on, holding onto wheelchairs; provide extra space for movement activities*
- *Instrument adaptations (Velcro, thicker mallets) may be needed for success in grasping*
- *Choose instruments of appropriate size and weight for physical condition of students*
- *Provide storage of equipment at appropriate height for physically challenged students*

Autism

The most recent evidence shows that 1 in 150 school-aged children suffers from an autism spectrum disorder. Autistic Spectrum Disorders (ASD) include Autism, Rett's, Childhood Disintegrative Disorder, Asperger's, and Pervasive Developmental Disorder Not Otherwise Specified (PDD-NOS). Whatever the diagnosis, these children have impairments in communication and social skills. Some are nonverbal, but many others are highly verbal yet have difficulty with the meaning or interpretation of language. The Autism Society of America has identified the following characteristics (not all of which will be apparent in all instances) of children on the autism spectrum: unresponsive to verbal cues, difficulty interacting with peers, repetition of words or phrases, difficulty communicating or expressing needs, oversensitivity or undersensitivity to pain or other stimuli, resistant to change, minimal eye contact, odd or unusual play—often sustained play or attachment to inanimate objects.

Tips for Improving Access:

- *Use visual schedules and other pictures to show daily routine**
- *Alert students when routine will be changing*
- *Maintain eye contact with student even though they may not seem to be responding*
- *Avoid over-stimulation from bright lights, loud sounds, or odors*
- *Communicate with classroom teacher regarding what works best with a particular student*
- *Provide alternative music experiences when possible*
- *Incorporate movement activities with music to improve gait and develop muscle coordination*

*An excellent source for visuals of all types is *Boardmaker* software available on the Internet at http://www.mayer-johnson.com/MainBoardmaker.aspx?MainCategoryID=5419.

Traumatic Brain Injury

Sometimes referred to as acquired brain injuries, traumatic brain injuries are caused by sudden force that is applied to the head, resulting in total or partial brain damage. Injuries from automobile accidents, falls, assaults, and sports injuries are the most common causes. Traumatic brain injury implies that the damage occurs in more than one part of the brain. Therefore, cognitive, physical, and behavioral abilities can be affected. Cognitive symptoms may include short or long-term memory loss, inability to make decisions, short attention span, and difficulty in communication. Physical symptoms may include fatigue, frequent headaches, seizures, lack of motor coordination, and sleeping disorders. Behavioral symptoms such as irritability, mood swings, and denial of the disability may also accompany the injury and students may have difficulty in establishing social skills such as relating to, and interacting with others.

Tips for Improving Access:

- *Use positive reinforcement when gains are made*
- *Limit distractions in the classroom*
- *Tailor adaptations to individual needs*
- *Reinforce conceptual information with aural or visual cues to aid memory*
- *Allow students to respond orally if they cannot do so in writing*
- *Use color-coding to simplify music notation*
- *Allow ample time for students to respond to questions or perform music tasks*

Learning Disabilities

Learning disabilities, which can range from mild to severe, result in significant difficulties in listening, speaking, reading, writing, reasoning, and/or mathematical ability. Students with learning disabilities have difficulty in interpreting, translating, or recalling information, resulting in a gap between their potential and their achievement. Most students with learning disabilities have normal intelligence, but have difficulty learning sequences of tasks. Students with learning disabilities may exhibit deficits in any of the following areas: visual-spatial motor tasks, processing information, language comprehension, social interaction, problem solving ability, paying attention and staying on-task. Although often identified as a learning disability, Attention Deficit Hyperactivity Disorder (ADHD) is actually a behavioral disorder.

Tips for Improving Access:

- *Realize that problems in processing information may lead to ineffective social skills*
- *Assist learning disabled students to determine how they learn best*
- *Use verbal reinforcement of rhythm patterns*
- *Use graphic notation if traditional notation is difficult*
- *Work on gross motor and fine motor skill development through playing instruments and movement activities*

Giftedness

There is not an agreed-upon definition of what constitutes giftedness. For many years the primary consideration for defining gifted students was based on intelligence alone, normally requiring an IQ score of 120 to 125 or above. The definition has been expanded recently to include children of unusual talent and creative ability. Current definitions range from students whose potential places them in the top 2 to 5 % of students of the same age, to students who show potential for performing at remarkably high levels of accomplishment when compared to others of their age, experience, or environment. The federal definition, as set forth in the No Child Left Behind legislation, defines gifted students as those "who give evidence of high achievement capability in . . . intellectual, creative, artistic, or leadership capacity . . . and who need services or activities not ordinarily provided by the school in order to fully develop those capabilities."[7]

Gifted students welcome challenging assignments such as research projects. They tend to relate with adults more readily than with peers so may need to be reminded to be cooperative when doing group work. Often, gifted students enjoy having leadership roles in the classroom, but teachers need to be careful that they are giving all students equal opportunities and not favoring gifted students unduly.

Historically, gifted students have often been promoted to a higher grade than their same age peers. This often results in social problems. A more preferred approach is to provide accelerated work and enrichment projects for the gifted

---

[7] *No Child Left Behind Act of 2001.* (Public Law 107-110), Title IX, Part A Section 9101(22), p. 544.

students. Large school districts and many colleges and universities offer enrichment classes and activities for gifted and talented students.

Tips for Improving Access:

- ♪ *Remember that gifted students are generally gifted in selected areas, not all areas*
- ♪ *Gifted students tend to be less conforming; may become bored easily*
- ♪ *Provide accelerated or enrichment work: research projects, extra readings, software composition programs, etc.*
- ♪ *Let them choose from a list of alternatives and/or encourage them to suggest options for further study*
- ♪ *Select them to be group leaders when appropriate*

Summary

Regardless of how special education students are categorized and labeled, it is important to remember that every student is unique and comes to school with individual characteristics and attributes. The music teacher's primary role is to modify and adapt the curriculum to meet children's individual needs while promoting social growth and aesthetic response to music whenever possible.

References

Access and Opportunities: A Guide to Disability Awareness. Washington, D.C.: VSA arts, 2006.

Ademek, Mary S., and Alice-Ann Darrow. *Music in Special Education.* 2nd ed. Silver Spring, MD: The American Music Therapy Association, 2010.

Bernstorf, Elaine, and Betty Welsbacher. "Helping Students in the Inclusive Classroom." *Music Educators Journal*, 82, no. 5 (March 1996).

Hackett, Patricia, and Carolynn A. Lindeman. *The Musical Classroom: Background, Models, and Skills for Elementary Teaching.* 8th ed. Upper Saddle River, NJ: Pearson Prentice Hall, 2009.

Hammel, Alice, and Ryan Hourigan. *Teaching Music to Students with Special Needs: A Label-Free Approach.* NY: Oxford Press, 2011.

Hunt, N., and K. Marshall. *Exceptional Children and Youth: An Introduction to Special Education.* 5th ed. Boston: Houghton Mifflin, 2013.

MENC. *Spotlight on Making Music with Special Learners.* Reston, VA: MENC, The National Association for Music Education, 2004.

Classroom Instruments 11

The playing of classroom instruments has long been a feature of elementary music programs in the elementary grades. The second of the nine National Standards for Music Education is "Performing on instruments, alone and with others, a varied repertoire of music." Many of the earliest experiences with instruments in general music involve using rhythm instruments such as rhythm sticks, tambourines, hand drums, claves, finger cymbals, and so forth. Experiences with Orff instruments can also be incorporated in the early grades. Bars on the Orff instruments are removable, allowing teachers to select instrument activities that require only 1, 2 or 3 notes.

Recorder

Recorder instruction often begins in the third or fourth grade and is used not only for music making, but also as an aid in learning to read standard music notation (National Standard #5), as well as for experiences with improvisation (National Standard #3). Unlike the flutophone, the recorder is an authentic instrument dating back to the fourteenth century. A full family of recorders, (soprano, alto, tenor, and bass) called a recorder consort, was often featured in polyphonic music of the Renaissance and Baroque eras.

Music educators began using the recorder as a part of elementary music instruction in the 1960s. The Orff approach uses recorders to add *ostinati* or improvisations to songs. The teacher would play these portions for students in grades K-2 and students could play simple ostinati beginning in grade 3.

Recorder Fingering Diagrams

Each oval in the fingering diagrams represents a hole on the recorder. The holes above the horizontal line are to be covered by the fingers and thumb of the left hand, and those below the line are for the right hand. A filled oval indicates that the hole is to be covered. Therefore, in the diagram below, the thumb and fingers one, two, and three of the left hand cover holes, but none of the fingers of the right hand cover holes since the ovals are not filled.

The fingering diagram represents the note "G" (second line of the treble clef). When playing the recorder it is essential that only a small stream of air is used, especially for lower pitches; otherwise, "over-blowing" will occur, resulting in a pitch an octave higher than desired.

"G"

Begin each note by whispering the word "do" (dew) into the instrument.

1.

do   do   do   do   etc.

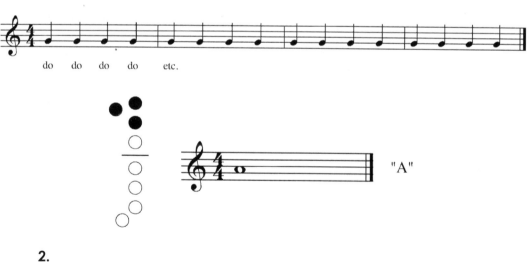

"A"

2.

3.

"B"

4.

5.

Lightly Row

6.

7.

"E"

8.

9.

10.

"D"

11.

Old Dan Tucker

12.

13.

"F"

14.

15.

16.

17.

18.

19.

"C"

20.

21.

22.

23.

24.

Kumbahya

25.

"C"

26.

27.

28.

Round

29.

Note Review

The Riddle Song

Ahrihagn

34.

Fine

D.C. al Fine

*Canon (one measure behind)

"B flat"

35.

Canon

36.

I Saw Three Ships

37.

"F sharp"

38.

"E"

39.

40.

Guitar

The guitar has several advantages over the piano as an accompanying instrument for elementary music classrooms. The piano tends to be quite loud and can easily cover children's voices. The students cannot see the teacher as clearly if the teacher is behind the piano. The guitar provides much better eye contact for the students and the teacher than the piano. Many children prefer the sound of the guitar to the piano. In addition to the teacher playing the guitar for the class, students in grade five and higher enjoy learning to play the guitar as well. The examples that follow use easy versions of chords when possible which allow students to learn more quickly.

Parts of the Guitar

The six **tuning pegs** at the top of the neck can be tightened or loosened to properly tune the six strings of the guitar The guitar is tuned primarily in fourths (except from the third string to the second which is a minor third) with letter names from the sixth string (the one closest to the upper body) to the first string being E, A, D, G, B, and E. The **neck** of the guitar is the fingerboard. The **nut** is the plastic piece at the upper end of the neck. Metal lines known as **frets**, which help determine the placement of the fingers, divide the neck. From one fret to the next represents a half step. In order to play in tune, fingers needed to create a chord should be placed near the fret without actually touching the fret.

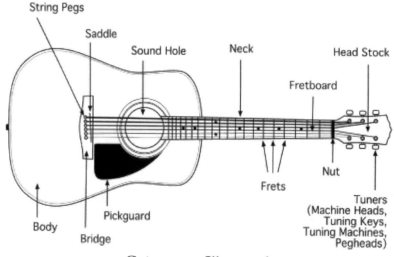

Guitar parts Illustrated

Playing Position

The guitar rests on the left knee with the neck slightly tilted up. The right forearm helps support the body of the guitar and the right hand is placed over the sound hole. The left hand thumb is placed on the back of the neck, near the nut, for playing beginning chords. The left hand fingers are placed firmly on the strings indicated by the tablature for each chord and the right hand fingers are used for strumming the strings. The strings should be strummed over the **sound hole** of the instrument. It is often easiest for beginners to use the thumb when strumming downward. (Players wishing to strum with the left hand and chord with the right need to have the guitar restrung and then the guitar is held with the neck pointing to the right).

Guitar Tablature

Although the guitar is held over the left knee in a nearly horizontal position, the chord diagrams or **tablature** are written as though the guitar were held in a vertical position with the six strings represented by vertical lines (beginning with the sixth string on the left). The horizontal lines represent the frets and a dot indicates that a finger is to be placed near that fret on that particular string. An x above a string shows that it is not to be played as part of the chord.

For the example below, a simplified version of the **C chord**, the index finger would be placed on the second string, first fret. (When finger numbers are used, the index finger is number 1, the middle finger is 2, the ring finger is 3, and the "pinky" or little finger is 4). Strings that are marked with an X are not played so only the top three strings are sounded for the simplified C chord.

Simplified C

The simplified version of the **G7 chord** is played by the index finger on the first string, first fret. Four strings can be played, but beginners may want to use three until they get used to adding the fourth string.

Simplified G7

When you can easily change from C to G7, you are ready to play "Chumbara." Strum the strings on beats one and three of "Chumbara" as shown by the slash marks.

Chumbara

Chum-ba - ra, _____ chum-ba - ra chum-ba - ra, _____ chum-ba - ra chum-ba - ra, _____

_____ chum-ba - ra chum chum chum chum chum chum chum chum, Chum-ba - ra, _____ chum-ba-ra

chum-ba - ra, _____ chum-ba - ra chum-ba - ra, _____ chum-ba - ra chum, chum!

The simplified **G chord** is played, as shown, by placing the third (ring) finger at the first string, third fret. Again, only four strings are played.

Simplified G

"Worried Man Blues" uses the G and C chords. Strum as indicated by the slash marks.

Worried Man Blues

It takes a wor-ried man to sing a wor-ied song, It
takes a wor-ried man to sing a wor-ried song, It
takes a wor-ried man to sing a wor - ried song, I'm wor - ried
(Count 1 now, 2 3 4) But I won't be wor - ried long.

The **D7 chord** does not have a simplified position. The 1st finger is placed on the second string, first fret (as in the simplified C chord), the 2nd finger is placed on the third string, second fret, and the 3rd finger is placed on the first string, second fret. Practice shifting from the D7 chord to the G chord until it is comfortable and then play "The Hokey Pokey" and "Michael Finnegan."

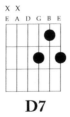

D7

Clementine

Michael Finnegan

Children's Game Song

The **E minor chord (Em)** uses all six strings. The 2ⁿᵈ finger is placed on the 5ᵗʰ string, second fret, and the 3ʳᵈ finger is placed on the fourth string, second fret.

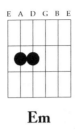

Em

The **B7 chord** employs all 4 fingers of the left hand. The 1ˢᵗ finger is on the 4ᵗʰ string, first fret; the 2ⁿᵈ finger on the fifth string, second fret; the 3ʳᵈ finger on the third string, second fret; and the 4ᵗʰ finger on the first string, first fret.

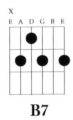

B7

Haida

Israel

Autoharp

Another instrument useful for elementary music is the autoharp. The autoharp has buttons, which produce a chord when depressed while the autoharp is strummed. A series of felt dampers mute the strings that are not a part of the chord. The most common autoharp models have either 15 or 21 different chords. Autoharps tend to need frequent tuning if not used regularly. Any of the previous songs for guitar can be accompanied on the autoharp. For kindergarten and first grade students, the teacher can depress the buttons while the children strum to the beat. Second grade and older children can learn to accompany songs with the autoharp fairly easily. It is also possible, though much more difficult, to use the autoharp as a melody instrument.

21 Button Autoharp

Piano

One of the most used instruments in music classrooms is the piano or electronic keyboard. Many children have portable keyboards in their homes and it is not unusual for elementary schools to have a keyboard lab or MIDI stations with keyboards. A keyboard can assist classroom teachers and/or students to play the melody of a song, add ostinatos to a song, play chords, or add a full accompaniment to a song.

As explained in Chapter 3, the keyboard is designed so that the black keys function both as a flat (lowered step) or a sharp (raised step) depending on the key of the song. A diagram of the arrangement of the keys on a keyboard is shown below.

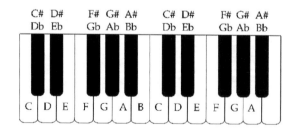

Many children's songs and other folk songs can be played in what is known as a five-finger pattern or position. The melody of a song is normally played with the right hand. The right hand thumb is numbered as finger 1, the index finger is 2, the middle finger is 3, the ring finger is 4, and the little finger is 5. The fingers should be curved over the keys.

The five finger pattern in the key of F Major, has the thumb on F, 2nd finger on G, 3rd finger on A, 4th finger on Bb, and the 5th finger on C. Use the F position as shown for the following pieces.

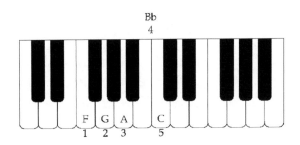

A Hunting We Will Go

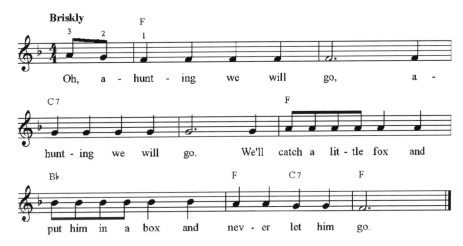

Oh, a - hunt - ing we will go, a -
hunt - ing we will go. We'll catch a lit - tle fox and
put him in a box and nev - er let him go.

Lightly Row

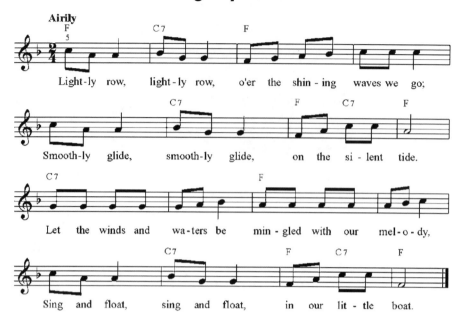

Light-ly row, light-ly row, o'er the shin - ing waves we go;

Smooth-ly glide, smooth-ly glide, on the si - lent tide.

Let the winds and wa-ters be min - gled with our mel-o - dy,

Sing and float, sing and float, in our lit - tle boat.

APPENDIX A
MUSIC SYMBOLS

Symbol	Name	Description
	Staff	5 lines
	Great Staff	Two staves used together
	Treble Clef	Top staff of Great Staff
	Bass Clef	Bottom staff of Great Staff
	Bar Line	End of measure
	Measure	From one bar line to the next
	Repeat Signs	Repeat the music
D.S. al Coda 𝄉	D.S. (Dal Segno)	Go to the sign
D.C. al Coda	D.C. (Da Capo)	Go to the beginning
Fine	Fine	End
pp	Pianissimo	Very soft
p	Piano	Soft
mp	Mezzo Piano	Medium soft
mf	Mezzo Forte	Medium loud
f	Forte	Loud
ff	Fortissimo	Very loud
	Crescendo	Gradually louder
	Decrescendo	Gradually softer
rit. or ritard	Ritardando	Gradually slower
accel.	Accelerando	Gradually faster

Symbol	Name	Description
	Staccato	Short, detached notes
	Slur	Connect the notes, smooth
	Tie	Play 1st note and keep sounding through 2nd
	Fermata	Hold the note longer than normal
	Meter Signature	Top number indicates how many beats in measure, bottom number shows what kind of note gets a beat
♯	Sharp	Raise note 1/2 step
♭	Flat	Lower note 1/2 step
♮	Natural	Cancels any accidental currently applied to note

APPENDIX B
Answer Key

Chapter Two Worksheets

Notes and Rests Worksheet, page 15

Note values with corresponding rests.

Meter Worksheets, pages 16

A. The notes needed to complete each measure are shown below.

B. Correct bar lines are shown below.

C. Correct meter signatures are given below.

Chapter Three Worksheets

Note Names Worksheet, page 59

Treble clef note names are:

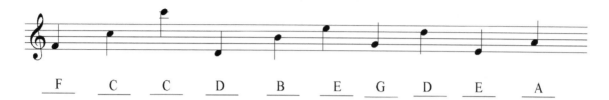

F   C   C   D   B   E   G   D   E   A

Bass clef note names are:

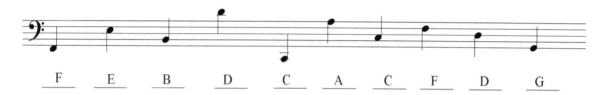

F   E   B   D   C   A   C   F   D   G

Half Steps and Whole Steps Worksheet page 60

The correct answers for whole or half steps are:

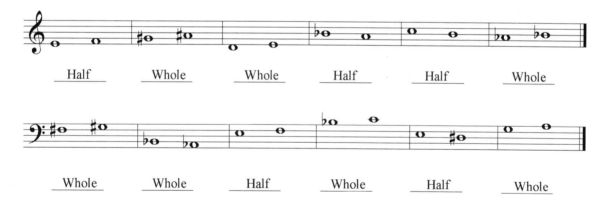

Half   Whole   Whole   Half   Half   Whole

Whole   Whole   Half   Whole   Half   Whole

Steps and Skips Worksheets, page 61

1. Steps, Skips, or Repeated notes are identified below:

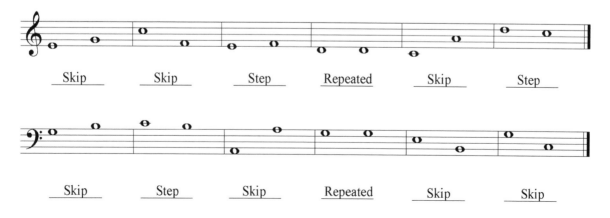

Skip   Skip   Step   Repeated   Skip   Step

Skip   Step   Skip   Repeated   Skip   Skip

2. Steps, Skips, and Repeated notes in "Somer Ade" are identified below.

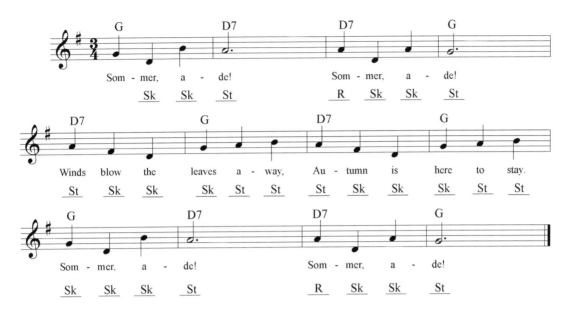

Solfege Worksheet, page 62

The correct Solfege names appear below each note.

Interval Worksheet, page 98

The correct intervals are shown below.

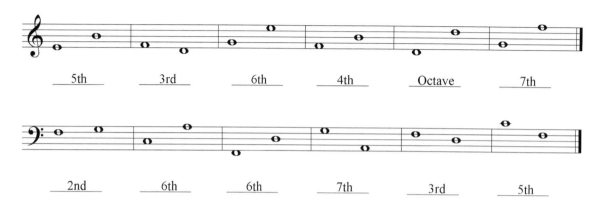

Major Scale Worksheet, page 63

The major scales are notated below.

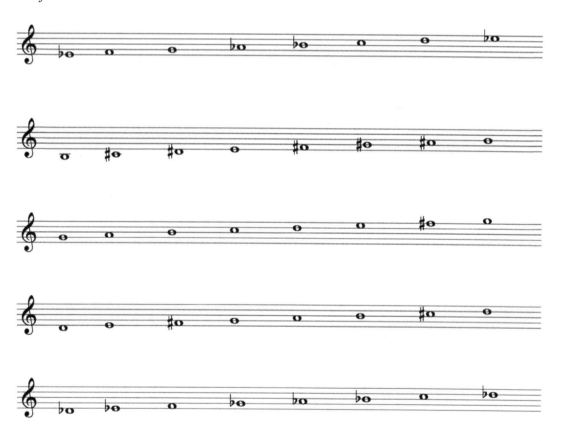

Major Scale Worksheet 2, page 64

Corrected versions of the scales are given below.

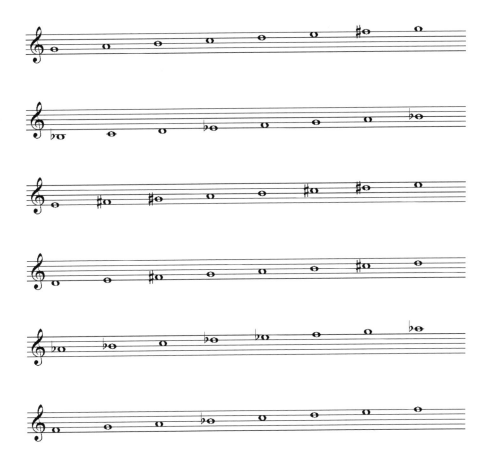

Key Signature Worksheet, page 65

The correct keys represented by the key signatures are shown below.

F   D   B   C

A♭   B♭   G♭

A   E   E♭

D   E♭   G

Chapter Four Worksheet

Chord Worksheet, page 105

1. The G and Db major scales with I, IV, and V chords are shown below.

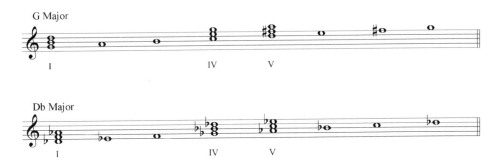

2. The triads below include the correct letter name of the chord and some have been altered so that all chords below are Major triads.

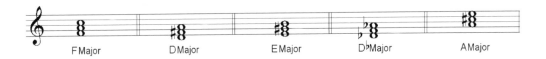

F Major   D Major   E Major   Db Major   A Major

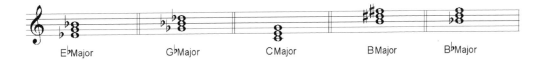

Eb Major   Gb Major   C Major   B Major   Bb Major

APPENDIX C
MUSIC CONCEPT INDEX*

Element/Concept	Streaming Clip#	Song/Activity Title	Page(s)
RHYTHM			
Steady Beat	2:1	"Clap Your Hands"	19
	2:2	"A Sailor Went to Sea"	20
	2:3	"Stamping Land"	21
	2:4a and b	"Jack-O'-Lantern"	23
	2:5	"Bee, Bee, Bumblebee"	25
	2:7	"The Elephant Song"	29
	2:8	"If You're Happy"	31
No Beat/Steady Beat	2:6	"The Wind Blew East"	27
Tempo			
Fast	2:8	"If You're Happy"	31
Slow	2:9	"Somer Ade"	33
Fast /Slow	2:10	"The Old Gray Cat"	35
Faster/Slower	2:11	"See the Pony Galloping"	36
Duration			
Ta and ti ti	2:4c	"Jack-O'-Lantern"	23
	2:12a and b	"Bye Baby Bunting"	38
	2:13	"Rover"	39
	2:16	"Rain is Falling Down"	43
	2:17	"Music Man"	45
Quarter rest	2:14	"Pease Porridge Hot"	40
	2:15a and b	"Bow Wow Wow"	41
Meter			
2's and 3's	2:18 a and b	"Meter in 2's or 3's"	46
Irregular Meter	2:19	"Speech Canon"	47
Syncopation	2:20	"My Landlord"	50
MELODY			
High and Low	3:1a and b	"Higher Than a House"	66
Melodic Direction			
Get Higher	3:2a and b	"This Old Man"	68
Get Lower	3:3	"Skin and Bones"	70
Higher and Lower	3:4	"Hot Dog Song"	72
	3:5	"Fleas"	74

*Many of the songs can be used for multiple concepts. This index indicates the main focus of the song as used in the lesson plans.

Element/Concept	Streaming Clip#	Song/Activity Title	Page(s)
So-Mi Songs	3:6	"See-Saw"	75
	3:7	"Star Light"	76
	3:8a and b	"The Counting Song"	77
	3:9a and b	"Clap Your Hands"	78
So-Mi-La Songs	3:10a and b	"Rain, Rain"	80
	3:11a	"Lucy Locket"	81
	3:12a and b	"Snail, Snail"	82
	3:13 Video	"Doggie, Doggie"	83
	3:14a and b	"Bounce High, Bounce Low"	85
	3:15	"Bye Baby Bunting"	86
	3:16a, b, and c	"Wee Willie Winkie"	87
Mi-Re-Do Song	2:17	"Rain Is Falling Down"	43
Do-Re-Mi-So Song	3:17a, b, and c	"Let Us Chase the Squirrel"	89
Pentatonic Song	3:18	"Great Big House"	90
Steps and Skips	3:20	"Scotland's Burning"	94
Major Scale	3.21a and b	"Scotland's Burning"	94
Curwen Hand Signs	3:9b	"Clap Your Hands"	78
	3:10b	"Rain, Rain"	80
	3:17c	"Let Us Chase the Squirrel"	89
	3:18b	Great Big House"	90
	3:21b	"St. Paul's Steeple"	95
Moveable Do	3:16 a, b, and c	"Wee Willie Winkie"	87
HARMONY			
Round (Canon)	4:1a and b	"Row, Row, Row Your Boat"	106
Descant	4:2	"The Three Rogues"	108
Two-part Singing	4:3	"America"	110
Chords (12 Bar Blues)	4:4	"Joe Turner Blues"	112
DYNAMICS			
Forte and Piano	3:16a, b, and c	"Wee Willie Winkie"	87

APPENDIX D
INDEX OF SONGS

Song Title	Page Number